CASHING IN ON NEEDLECRAFTS

CASHING IN ON NEEDLECRAFTS

Jennifer Curry

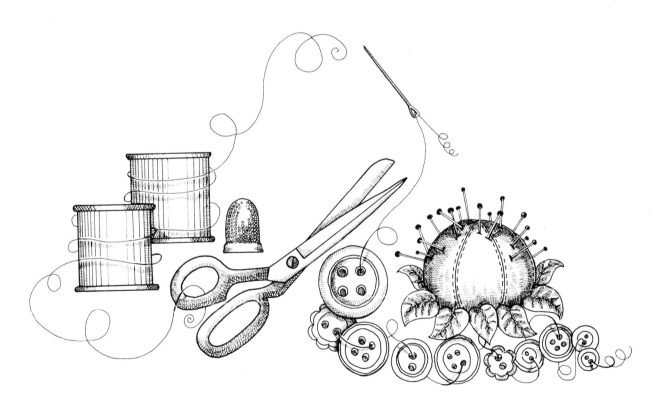

DAVID & CHARLES

Newton Abbot   London   North Pomfret (Vt)

AUTHOR'S NOTE

Most of the 'craftspeople' or 'craftspersons' I spoke to while working on this book were women. Without exception they called themselves 'craftsmen'. Some held office in so-called Guilds of Craftsmen which numbered more women than men among their members, yet saw nothing inappropriate in their guild's name. I became very confused. 'Nowadays,' I remonstrated, 'we are supposed to call women "women" and men "men".' 'It doesn't matter what we're *called*,' they retorted. 'What matters is what we *do*.'

So there I left it. Throughout the following pages the people who practise crafts have been referred to at random as craftspeople, craftsmen and craftswomen regardless of their sex and according to my mood of the moment rather than any considered policy. I apologise in advance for any irritation it may cause but remain unrepentant. Mere names must always take second place to people, and this was the people's choice.

JC

Colour photography (unless specified otherwise) by Tony Griffiths, Photography 2000'

Illustrations by Jennifer Johnson

Wedding dress designs on pp105-6 by Margot Graville

All letterheads, logos, designs, labels etc reproduced in this book are copyright of the individual craftspeople and must not be reproduced in any way without prior permission from the copyright holder

British Library Cataloguing in Publication Data

Curry, Jennifer
  Cashing in on needlecrafts.
  1. Textile crafts——Marketing
  I. Title
  746'.068'8   TT699

  ISBN 0–7153–8663–9
  ISBN 0–7153–8742–1 Pbk

Typeset by ABM Typographics Ltd Hull and printed in Great Britain By Butler & Tanner Ltd, Frome and London for David & Charles (Publishers) Limited Brunel House   Newton Abbot   Devon

Published in the United States of America by David & Charles Inc North Pomfret   Vermont 05053   USA

Contents

This book is dedicated, with love and gratitude,
to our good friends, Tom and Fanny

Introduction

We live in a period when the machine rules our lives and manufactured, mass-produced goods are relatively cheap to buy, attractive to look at, and easy to care for. Walk through any multiple chain store and you will find sweaters, dresses, woollen scarves and caps, toddlers' jump-suits — a whole range of fabric goods that are bright, colourful, well designed and affordable.

For anyone wanting to earn money through needlecrafts this can be a daunting sight. How is it possible to compete? How can any individual hope to charge prices that realistically reflect the hours of skilled work required to create hand-made goods and still find willing customers?

The answer is simple. People are tired of faceless machines. Good, careful, creative craftsmen can always find customers prepared to pay for their skills because there is a longing for the personal touch, the individuality, the 'something special' that hand-made items possess and which cannot possibly be matched by goods churned out in their hundreds and thousands.

When I was writing *Cooking for Cash* I discovered that those who enjoyed food were prepared to pay almost twice as much for a special dish, such as Coq au Vin or Boeuf Bourguignonne, made by a freelance cook than for an apparently identical one which they could pick up from the deep-freeze of any reputable supermarket. It seemed illogical but it was a fact. What they were paying for was, quite literally, the human touch. The sprinkle of seasoning instead of the carefully controlled measurement; the dash of herbs and spices; the zest of peel or juice added according to the cook's mood rather than the dictates of the recipe. Just imagine the flavour of home-made vegetable soup of the 'bung-it-all-in-the-pot' variety compared with shop-bought vegetable soup and you can almost conjure up in your mind the difference in taste and quality.

It's the same sort of difference that makes the craftsman-made garment, toy or soft-furnishing such a coveted item. When I ran my own craft shop one of my most popular lines was a tiny teddy bear which sold for just under £2. The toymaker delivered two dozen teddies every Friday and invariably they had all been sold by Saturday afternoon. Charming though they were, I never totally understood their huge popularity until one of my customers pointed out that no two bears had the same expression on their faces. They were all individuals. Each had his own mood and personality, and each reflected the mood and personality of the toymaker. *That's* the sort of difference that people are prepared to pay for, whether it is expressed in a soft toy, a hand-made tie, a patch-work skirt, a lace-trimmed petticoat, a cushion, a draught-excluder, or whatever.

There is also a market for things created especially for customers' individual requirements: made-to-measure clothes; bedspreads and curtains to match their bedroom colour scheme; fabric murals to enhance a particular corner of their living-room.

And this is an exciting thought for people in all sorts of circumstances created by the society we live in. For anyone who cannot find employment, for the advertising executive who has been made redundant, for the divorced woman struggling to bring up a young family, for those who are housebound by the demands of children or aged relatives, or by disablement, age or illness — for all of these, and more, there is the opportunity to make an independent income.

The truth is that if you are prepared to combine individuality with a high standard of design and craftsmanship, and if you are prepared to be business-like both in your making and your marketing methods, then you too can cash in on needlecrafts and make money from an activity that will give you both pleasure and satisfaction.

1 Check Your Skills

Before you launch into the business of attempting to earn money by cashing in on needlecrafts there are a few basic questions you should ask yourself. The first, and by far the most important, is: 'Do I positively enjoy this activity?' There is no point at all in spending hours crouched over patterns, needles and pins if it gives you no pleasure. To start with, there are other ways of earning money, even in these days of high unemployment. Secondly, in a very strange way, crafts created reluctantly do not seem to possess the sparkle or give the pleasure that shines off them if they have been created with zest and enjoyment. It is a common phenomenon. Cooks, carpenters, nurses, shop assistants, journalists and jobbing gardeners — all seem to produce better work from a contented mind.

So, if you've said 'No' to the first question, read no further. If yours is a skill which does give you genuine pleasure, there are other questions that need honest answers.

Practical Skills and Creative Imagination

Am I a good craftsman, prepared to work to high standards and a perfect finish?

Is there one particular item — a sweater, perhaps — that I can make very well?

Are there other items — such as hats, scarves, gloves, leg-warmers — that I can make to vary the application of my skill if fashion, taste and the market changes, or if I get bored as a result of making just one type of item, or if I can't make enough money from just one item?

If at present I do not feel sufficiently skilled to sell what I make, have I the energy, will and opportunity to improve my skills, either by teaching myself with the help of books and TV courses, by going to regular classes, or by enrolling for weekend or summer schools?

Can I produce a particular item in large numbers and in a comparatively short time — say, sixty soft toys each week — or am I happier working more slowly, to individual order only?

Have I sufficient imagination and flair for design to create my own models and patterns, or do I need to use other people's designs?

Have I sufficient visual sense to present my work so that buyers and potential customers find it extremely attractive and desirable at first glance?

Have I the practical ability to make things that will stand up well to use, wear, tear and cleaning, rather than just look good? (People will buy the first time because of appearance, but only if their purchase goes on giving pleasure and does not shed its buttons or trimmings, come apart at the seams, begin to sag, or fade, or fray, or develop lumpy bumps, will they buy a second time or recommend you to their friends.)

Temperament and Fitness

Am I sufficiently well disciplined to cope with the boredom of repeating the same item again and again, or would the production of, say, fifteen matinée jackets weekly drive me wild?

Am I sufficiently well disciplined to work when I don't really want to, or when I feel tired or off-colour, in order to fill orders on time?

Am I sufficiently confident to carry on working even when the orders are not coming in and no one seems to be interested in what I have to sell? Can I stand the insecurity and irregularity of freelance work, or would I prefer a regular job?

Am I tough enough to take a strong stand when I have to face unpleasant problems — such as a customer who will not pay his/her debts; or a supplier who does not provide urgently required materials in the promised quantities, at the promised price, or at the promised time; or a buyer who gives an order and then changes his/her mind when the work is practically complete?

Do I like the idea of working on my own, or do I need other people for comfort, companionship, encouragement and moral support?

If I prefer to be part of a group do I want to be on equal terms with the others; take orders; or give orders?

Have I the courage and self-confidence to sell my own product, or would I need to appoint an agent or find a partner to do the selling for me?

Am I fit enough to cope with the demands of producing sufficient goods to fill my order book? (This is rather a question of stamina than perfect health for home crafts and 'outwork' can fit in well with the special problems of the disabled.)

Organisational Ability

Am I able to organise myself and other people? Does a crisis enthuse or panic me?

Am I sufficiently cool-headed to juggle my time and activity and concentration so that all the different processes of a craft business — buying materials, making goods, marketing goods, delivering goods, and so on — can all progress simultaneously?

Can I cope with the business side of freelance craft-selling — buy at the right prices, organise my cash flow, cost my product and my time sensibly? If not, am I willing and able to learn?

Can I find the money, if necessary, for a certain amount of capital investment in equipment and materials and transport, as well as whatever is required for advertising? Do I need to find extra work space?

Do I want to earn my living, or am I simply interested in developing a profitable hobby?

It is a very useful exercise to go through these questions, putting your personal answers together to make a profile of the sort of craftsman you are, what stage you have reached, what your potential is, and what direction you want to take. During my research I interviewed Jean Tenny who wrote the following profile for me when she was just about to launch herself into business. She was a competent, amateur needlewoman who had had the idea of selling made-to-measure school uniforms and leisure-wear to the four schools in the district where she lived, and also of doing alterations and repairs to children's clothes, perhaps in conjunction with the school exchange shop.

> I am a good, careful craftsman, experienced in making and altering children's clothes of all types, primarily for my own sons and daughter but also for lots of nephews and nieces and the children of my friends. During the winter I am going to enrol at the local college to do an evening class once a week in Advanced Dressmaking because I think I might learn one or two tips that could make me faster and more efficient. I can produce a lot of work these days because all my children are at school now and my husband is away a lot so I have masses of time to myself. I am not particularly imaginative, certainly not a designer, so I intend to stick to basic uniform and casual gear — tough and hard-wearing — or I will follow patterns parents bring me.
>
> I reckon there is enough variety in what I am hoping to do to stop me from being bored and to keep me working, and since everyone says nice things

9

about the clothes I make for my own children I doubt whether I shall lose confidence now. I've been doing it too long — my eldest child is 14. I would be nervous about taking on a customer who didn't pay but I shall always ask for either the materials or the cost of the materials to be provided in advance, so the most I can lose is the cost of my time. I don't really think many parents with children at local schools would risk their reputations by running up debts or making trouble — but I suppose there just could be the odd one. I'll just have to learn to cope with that if and when it crops up and hope that I'll be brave!

I like working with people and am hoping to have two partners for that reason — it could be very lonely just sitting at home working away on your own every day. I've found two friends to go in with me — one is a demon knitter and will probably specialise in knitwear, the other is particularly good at difficult things like trousers and tailored shorts, so I'll be concentrating on shirts, blouses and dresses, but I hope we'll all help each other when necessary and share the work, responsibility and profits. None of us is confident about the actual selling side but I imagine we'll boost each other's morale — I'm sure I could sell Joffy's knitwear better than she could and she's always the greatest fan of my little print dresses. I hope that the school notice boards, and parents' recommendation, and the children *wearing* the clothes, will do the selling for us.

We're all still pretty young and active so I think we've got enough stamina — most of the time anyway — but I can get panicked by a crisis, especially if I have problems at home with one of the children ill, or something like that. That's another reason for wanting a group of three — we can help each other to keep calm and get through all the work and organisation. I know I wouldn't be able to cope with everything single-handed. Anyway, I'm hoping to make my customers do some of the work by bringing me their own materials and patterns whenever possible, and the actual delivery of the goods will be simplified if I can arrange to have things picked up from the schools. I have good contacts with all the schools since at least one of my children has spent some time at each of them, and so have my friends' kids, and we've been on the Parent Teacher Associations and things like that, so we're all pretty well known and I think the staff will co-operate.

I'm not very good at business, but Joffy is married to an accountant and he's going to talk to us about costing and keeping books and things. Otherwise I would have paid for a session of advice from an accountancy firm, I think, and talked to a bank manager. There's no point if we're not going to make at least a bit of money, so we do need to know how to work out that side of things. We'll be working from our own homes so we don't need premises, and we have three perfectly good sewing-machines and a knitting-machine among us, plus a couple of cars, so I really don't think we'll need any capital to get started — if we do we'll get a floater from our husbands and pay it back when we start earning. The first profits will go into an account for the business anyway, as a sort of safety belt, or umbrella, just in case we suddenly need to spend money. We might need a new machine — an overlocker perhaps because I've been told they're wonderful and save hours of time. That could be a good investment — *when* or *if* we have money to invest. But we do want to start small and be cautious, because none of us has a lot of money to play about with. At present we're only thinking about making a part-time income, but I would like to think that when my kids left home I could make it into a full-time one. Partly because I'd like to feel that I *could* be self-supporting, as a matter of pride. Partly because you hear of so many men being made redundant, and of so many couples being divorced, that you never know when you might just *have* to be self-supporting.

You probably haven't got to the stage of thinking out a crafts business idea in as much detail as Jean had, but by the time you have answered the questions and really thought through your aims and objectives you should have some idea of what type of money-making venture would most appeal to you — whether it would be a small, single-handed interest demanding only limited time and resources, or whether it would be an ambitious project in which you would invest money and perhaps employ staff. You should also have some idea of whether you are already sufficiently skilled to produce marketable goods at a realistic price, sell them effectively and deliver them on time.

If you want to earn in this way, feel that you have the flair and the aptitude, but are not completely confident of your skills either as a craftsman or as a business tycoon, then there are various ways in which you can improve your skills. The method you choose will probably depend upon the time and the money you have available, but the facilities are just waiting to be used.

2 Extend Your Skills

Anyone who wants to learn more and to develop his/her skills can do so. It just needs time and determination. Sometimes it also needs money, but occasionally it is possible to be paid while you are being trained.

The Library

First of all you should make a bee-line for the largest library you can find, and rummage through those shelves laden with books dealing with Crafts and Business Organisation. All the books will be indexed and those you are looking for will have their spines numbered as follows:

Making an income from a business — books beginning with the number 331
Organisation, accountancy and marketing — books beginning with 658
Practical crafts, things to make — books beginning with 646
Design and the more artistic, creative side of needlecrafts — books beginning with 745 and 746

This numbering takes it for granted that your library uses the Dewey Decimal system of indexing

because I never come across a library that uses any other these days. Note that the first three digits show the *main* subject matter, the numbers that follow the decimal point indicate the various sub-divisions. If you run into difficulties don't hesitate to ask the librarian for assistance and advice. Most of them are only too anxious to be helpful and know their stock very well, so even if you can't find what you want on their display they may know that there's an appropriate book in the reference department, or tucked away in their reserve stock, or available from a nearby library, or temporarily out on loan but able to be ordered. They'll also help you to get to grips with their filing system, microfiche information screens and computer print-outs, and though this may all sound and look very frightening to the newcomer it's really quite simple once you get the hang of it, as well as being much less time-consuming than having to search shelf after shelf.

You can teach yourself an amazing amount from books. Here's a reader's letter to *Popular Crafts* that tells its own story.

Dear Editor,

I felt that I just had to write to tell you how success-ful I have been making the soft toys from the *Soft Toy Collection.*

I bought it on impulse to make the Blue Whale. I had never made soft toys before and I thought it looked easy. I made it up in an afternoon and made a blue Rabbit with the bits left over. Encouraged by my success I went on to make the Poodle for my Mother who has one (a real one) very similar. She of course showed it to her Poodle-loving friends and I was inundated with orders for Christmas. I have made him in several colours and also trimmed him to match the owner's original poodle fashion trim. I followed the instructions for pricing toys, and I am pleased to say I made quite a nice little profit. I am now thinking of taking a stand at a craft show later in the year. Please convey my thanks to June Johnson Smith — I only wish I had tried toymaking years ago.

Mrs Joyce Janes, Dartford, Kent.
From *Popular Crafts,* March 1984.

The *Soft Toy Collection,* and many other useful and attractive books, are listed in Appendix 1.

For the most part it's wise to make sure that any books you use are reasonably modern and up to date. Both craft-making designs and techniques as well as business methods tend to move rapidly with the times, so you need to know what's new. On the other hand it is some-times possible to get some attractive and un-usual visual ideas from browsing through old designs, provided that you can work out how to adapt and re-create them by using contempor-ary methods and materials, or can find a market for nostalgic bygones. The latter is quite a lucra-tive avenue to research if you are looking for an unusual product to sell. For example, Victorian-style clothes, especially underclothes and nightdresses in real cotton or linen, are in great demand again, as well as old-fashioned patch-work quilts, and thirties-style silk lingerie, rag dolls and flappers' beachwear from the roaring twenties have all made a come-back. Many cults and passions from the past lie dormant for fifty years or more and then come soaring back into fashion, whether they are things to wear, things to decorate or furnish our houses with, or things

for our children to play with. If you are clever or lucky enough to see the possibility of reviving an old fashion and re-creating it as a contemporary craze your business could turn into a gold-mine. Just think how Laura Ashley resuscitated old-fashioned prettiness and made it the vogue of the eighties.

The library will also have a magazine section where you can browse without having to buy — if you try this technique in a newsagent's shop the proprietor tends to lose patience after a while! Some magazines you will want to buy — there is a list of very useful ones in Appendix 2. Some you will just want to glance at from time to time. If you get to know what's available through scan-ning their contents in the library's reading-room first of all you will know which are the ones to spend your money on. Magazines *are* very ex-pensive now so you should only invest in the ones that are really going to help you to make money by giving you ideas and contacts.

This is also the place to find information about any useful societies or organisations in your area, and establishments which could provide you with extra training should you need it. The library will probably have leaflets about the facilities offered by your local College of Further Education. My own provides a staggering variety of craft courses, including: appliqué; patchwork and patchwork embroidery; quilting; crochet; making silk flowers; leathercraft; macramé; em-broidery — hand or machine, standard or ad-vanced, modern or traditional, creative, and gold or silver work; embroidering greetings cards; lacemaking; machine-knitting; needle-crafts — hand or sewing-machine; upholstery; soft furnishings; soft toys; spinning and dyeing; weaving; tapestry; making gifts.

There are also commercial courses including: book-keeping for small businesses; starting your own small business; and running your own small business.

Some of the classes are held during the day, some in the evening, and the fees are approxi-mately 60p per hour, so for a 10-week course of 2 hours a week the charge would be about £12 (by 1984 values) and that must surely represent a good investment of time and money.

The library may also have details about extra-mural classes or extension studies at the nearest art college or university, or information about local education authority vacation schemes, or advertisements about courses being held at arts centres and craft centres near you. It may direct you to the Women's Institute which is particularly interested not only in encouraging women to make crafts of a high standard, but also in helping women *and* men to sell crafts through its markets. The institute runs Denman College which organises residential courses in collage, patchwork, lacemaking, machine-knitting, and so on, as well as a course on selling through the WI (see Appendices 3 and 4).

For urban dwellers the Townswomen's Guilds, with their craft courses, lessons and demonstrations, will certainly be within striking distance, and will without doubt have something of interest in their programme. The National Secretary will be delighted to send you general information, as well as details of your local guild (see Appendix 3).

There may be a local group of the Quilters' Guild near you, since this young organisation, which has only been in existence for five years, is expanding, has several local groups and a panel of lecturers, and organises workshops all over the country, as well as carrying news in advance of courses and classes in its magazine, *The Quilters' Guild Newsletter*, available to members (see Appendix 3).

Embroiderers who take themselves seriously should think about becoming members of the Embroiderers' Guild which has many branches nationwide which organise lectures and events. Or you might like to make contact with the Royal School of Needlework which has a huge spread of courses available, ranging from the two-year full-time course to shorter day or evening courses covering such subjects as appliqué, drawn thread work, church embroidery and patchwork. Alternatively, get in touch with the Creative Needlecraft Association — another society which organises courses — and find out what they have to offer (see Appendix 3).

Knitting-machine clubs are sprouting up all over the country, often organised by the knitting-machine manufacturers, such as Knitmaster, but also by the well-respected Worldwide

Machine Knitters' Club, whose address is in Appendix 3.

There are also privately organised centres for craft courses, often based in the homes and studios of professional craftspeople who both make *and* teach. Many of these are advertised in the craft magazines, but the local library is the place to find out what your area has to offer.

The Bookshop and Newsagent

It is unlikely that you will want to do all your reading and research in the library. Sooner or later you will find that there are books and magazines that you want to keep by you for future reference. There are many specialist craft magazines which will be useful to you, not only for their articles, features and patterns, but also because of the small-ads section which will help you to find supplies of the materials and equipment you need through mail order. This tends either to be cheaper than retail shop prices, or it provides easy post-box shopping for those who are not able to travel far, or it offers a source of specialised equipment which is not easy to find in local or even large town and city shops. Many of the magazines also publish details of forthcoming craft markets, fairs, shows and exhibitions which have the three-fold advantage of providing you with a source of ideas, a range of contacts, and an outlet for your goods as soon as you are ready to start selling. Nor is it only the craft magazines that are useful. Practically every woman's magazine or household do-it-yourself magazine has a section devoted to the interests of the craftsman, knitting patterns, sewing patterns, kits, design suggestions, craft techniques, often outlined in step-by-step detail. Whether you want to transform your holiday snaps into embroidered pictures, create a knitted bedspread with cushions to match, dress a doll in the latest royal christening robe, or simply crochet a lampshade from a ball of string, some magazine, somewhere, has told you how, at some time. There are also pages and pages of well-illustrated examples of what's in fashion, what's new, smart, attractive and sellable, whether it's in the field of clothes, soft-furnishings, babywear, or babyware, toys, gifts and novelties. You may not want to copy them precisely, but they will keep your eyes open to contemporary design and start your brain ticking over with an abundance of related ideas that have been triggered off. (For useful magazines, both specialist and general, see Appendix 2.)

The craft magazines, and a few of the general interest ones, are one source of information about a pleasant way of brushing up your skills, and that is through special interest holidays. Not only are these advertised in the small-ad columns where you can find everything from picture-knitting weeks in rural Wales to carpet-weaving in the Greek Islands, but *Popular Crafts* has made it particularly easy by producing a *Guide to Special Interest Holidays*, obtainable from their Hemel Hempstead office. At a cost of £2.20 (1984 price) for 150 holidays this is probably money well spent and much easier than going along to your travel agent and combing the brochures for something that fits your particular bill.

The Jobcentre

Your next visit, if you are anxious for further training as an entry into a new career, could well be to the Jobcentre. Here the Manpower Services Commission TOPS adviser will give you details about government-funded retraining schemes which will equip you to make money from your latent skill. Courses available include 'Tailoring and Cutting' as well as 'Training for Self-Employment', though they vary from place to place depending upon local demand. The good thing about the TOPS scheme is that as yet the course is provided free and trainees are given a living allowance, and perhaps a travel and lunch allowance, as well as other supplements if they are eligible — though because of government cutbacks in spending this may not last more than a year or two and it is thought that soon trainees will have to pay towards their retraining. The Jobcentre staff will give you leaflets about 'Training Opportunities' in your area and about 'Allowances for TOPS Trainees'. They will, however, want to be quite sure that they are training you to work and earn, not simply to enjoy a profitable hobby.

Television

Television plays an important part in craft education, and careful study of the *Radio Times* and *TV Times* — especially in the autumn when people are often inclined to learn something new — will reveal several programmes devoted to dressmaking, knitting and other related creative pursuits. These tend to be very good, with skilled practitioners showing the tricks of their trade carefully, thoughtfully and in close-up. Often the courses are accompanied by books giving more detailed instruction than TV time allows, and the two together make a very effective teaching method. For instance, in the summer of 1984, the combination of the BBC1 series 'Quilting', combined with the BBC publication *Quilting, An Introduction to American Patchwork Design* by Penny McMorris, attracted a great deal of interest in this reborn craft. Details of the book are listed in Appendix 1.

Experience and Example

Often, though, we learn most through unofficial channels, through a sort of grapevine that craftspeople share. If you know of someone who has skills you would like to acquire, ask if you can watch him or her at work. A request of this sort is usually granted since it is, rightly, accepted as a genuine compliment rather than nosiness or interference. I remember watching a group of women in Downton sitting in fascination around the last lacemaker in Wiltshire who was making Downton lace. The old lady was 83; she knew that her time, and her eyesight, were running out, but the younger ones were determined that her craft should not die with her. As a result of the few months they spent together there are now lively young women in Downton and the surrounding area who can and do, once again, make Downton lace.

If you want to learn from someone else's experience you must be humble, no matter how skilled you may be in another field. You must watch, look, listen; use your head, your hands, your eyes; imitate and practise until you become perfect. It is a sort of do-it-yourself apprenticeship. One of the women I interviewed told me how she had become a skilled tailor and dressmaker. Though completely untrained she had managed to get a job in a theatre wardrobe on the strength of having made costumes for the university drama group when she was a philosophy student. In the theatre there was an old man who was a superb cutter and tailor, but a rather dour and withdrawn character who did not socialise with the rest of the theatre staff and was normally to be found working quietly in a corner on his own. Susie lost no time in getting to know him. Whenever she had time she was at his elbow, asking him exactly what he was doing, and why, and how. Gradually he unfolded the secrets of his trade, pleased to find someone who respected his craftsmanship. Painstakingly Susie practised and perfected what she learnt from him — and from then on there was no looking back. Now she is a highly skilled tailor and dressmaker who can make practically anything that any customer might dream up, no matter how complicated.

3 Basic Contacts

The Hobby Craftsman

For those interested only in needlecrafts as a profitable hobby, few contacts are necessary. It is a comparatively simple business to start making things for friends and neighbours who will provide or pay for materials, plus an extra fee for your time and skill. Knitting sweaters, sewing babyclothes or school uniforms, altering or creating clothes, especially outsize clothes or maternity wear, upholstering chairs, making curtains and matching bedspreads — there are usually lots of people who will willingly pay well to have jobs of this sort done for them. If you do them well word will get around like wildfire and you will never be short of work. At the most you will need a postcard advertisement in a local shop window just to get you started, but once you *are* started the main problem will not be to find work, but to prevent yourself from becoming totally inundated with orders. You need to be very firm about not taking on more than you can cope with, otherwise you may find you never have a spare moment for relaxation, or you could try to work in so much of a hurry that you

allow your standards to slip, or the work itself becomes a chore and drudgery rather than a pleasure. This is self-defeating. Avoid it by starting very gradually and building up slowly, pacing yourself so that you know how much you can take on in comfort, and never allowing yourself to be pushed beyond your self-imposed limit. If customers really want your skills they will be prepared to give their orders well in advance and then bide their time. In fact, they will value you more for knowing that your services are in demand and that you are sufficiently sure of yourself and what you have to offer to be able to say 'No', or 'Yes, but not yet', when work is crowding in on you.

The Outworker

If you are quite happy to be an outworker, home-based and working to someone else's requirements, there are only one or two contacts you will need to make apart from the initial one of finding someone to keep you in work and pay you a modest sum for it.

Local papers and craft magazines often carry

advertisements for outworkers of all kinds, often framed like this: 'Experienced sewing machinists required, working from home. Competitive prices per garment. Tel: 123 4567.'

If you are a knitter you might be able to make contacts through your local wool shops, asking the proprietor either to display an advertisement or mention your name to any of her customers she knows are knitting for profit and in bulk and need help.

Alternatively, if you are expert, you could write to Sirdar Ltd or Patons & Baldwins — you will find their addresses in Appendix 5. Both companies employ hundreds of outworkers but there are many people wanting to work for them so you may not be lucky at first. It may be that you will be put on a waiting list, or asked to repeat your request after six months or so. Or you may be asked to send a sample of your work for consideration. This is the sort of letter Patons sends to those who approach them at a time when they have vacancies.

Dear Ms Anyone,

We thank you for your communication concerning the possibility of your doing Home Knitting for us, and accordingly we shall be pleased to examine your work if you will send us garments of plain knitting and ribbing and lacy pattern. (Machine-Knitting is not acceptable as all our display garments must be hand knitted.) The garments need not be new but should be in good condition and they will be returned to you as soon as possible after examination, (small samples of this work are not suitable) but we should be interested to know if you can undertake Fair Isle Knitting and Crochet and small samples of these would be adequate.

We must point out that only the highest standard of work can be accepted. Knitting instructions, wool and needles would be supplied to you and Outworkers are asked to knit the fabric and return all pieces and unused wool to us for examination before the pieces are made up by our staff in the factory. A date is given for the return of the work and we ask for full co-operation in this as we ourselves have to work to a time schedule but we endeavour at all times to see that the time given is adequate, approximately 2/3 weeks for full size garments.

We shall look forward to hearing from you at your earliest convenience . . .

Similarly, J & P Coats gives work to embroiderers, crocheters, tatters and tapestry makers. They describe their operation in the following way.

We have a team of home workers making up new models to be photographed for publication in magazines or our own books. Many of the models are then used as display pieces in Needlecraft Shops. Needless to say we have to maintain a high standard of technique because they are continually in the public eye. Our work fluctuates according to our programme, and because of this we are unable to guarantee work on a regular basis — we can have very busy periods, alternatively quiet spells. We pay an hourly rate plus postage — occasionally set fees are offered.

Consideration will be given to applications on receipt of samples of work. We are particularly interested in workers for freestyle embroidery, but would like our workers to be versatile in all styles, if possible.

Outworking still thrives in this country, as it did even in the Middle Ages, because it is the easiest way of making money. There is no travelling, no leaving the family, no fitting in with other people's daily routine — the work can be slotted in with particular and individual commitments or restrictions, including disability. But just because it is so popular it tends to be severely underpaid and recently there have been moves to prevent the homeworker from being exploited for business profits. Consequently, before you get too involved, it would be wise to make contact with Homeworkers' Association of the Low Pay Unit, sending them a stamped addressed envelope and a request to know more about fair pay for the job, whether it is piecework or paid by the hour. You will find the address in Appendix 3. If you have been offered work but are not sure whether the conditions and rewards are fair you might like to get in touch with ACAS — the Advisory Conciliation and Arbitration Service — and discuss it with them. You can track them down either through your local telephone directory or through the Jobcentre or the Citizens' Advice Bureau.

Toymakers can find out all they need to know about rates of pay and payment of expenses by reading the guide to legislation in the industry as outlined in the Toy Manufacturers' Wages Order. Send for your free copy to the Department of Employment, at the address given in Appendix 3. In fact, this is a very useful document for all homeworkers because the guidelines laid down for toymakers can usefully be applied to other craftspeople. As from June 1983 it recommends a minimum hourly rate of £1.49 per hour. For piece-work, the average time taken to make a given object should be calculated and then increased by 10 per cent. So, if an article takes two hours to make, by a worker who is neither phenomenally fast nor extraordinarily slow, the payment should be twice the hourly payment of £1.49, which is £2.98, plus 10 per cent, which is approximately 30p, bringing the total to £3.28 and raising the hourly rate to £1.64. The sad truth is that a vast number of homeworkers consider themselves lucky to earn about half that.

Although it is unlikely that your income as an outworker will do very much to affect your tax position you should inform the local **Inspector of Taxes** that you are earning money. (You will find his address and telephone number in the telephone directory listed under Inland Revenue.) If you don't volunteer this information it's possible that your employer will, and enquiries will be made. If you are on a state pension you can supplement your income by your earnings, but these will be taxed if they go over the current limit. If in doubt, ask for advice, either at the tax office or the Citizens' Advice Bureau.

Finally, you should go along to the **Social Security Office** and explain that you are self-employed. You will be required to pay Class 2 National Insurance contributions unless your earnings are below the 'exception limit' which changes from year to year. Even if you could claim exception it may be worth paying contributions voluntarily since the benefits they confer at present include: sickness benefit; retirement pension; widow's benefit; maternity grant and allowance; child's special allowance. For married women the position can be quite complicated but a leaflet, 'NI.1 Married Women: Your National Insurance Position,' explains it all quite clearly. Leaflet 'NI.95' is for divorced women, leaflet 'NI.51' advises widows. It is wise to discuss your personal situation with one of the staff at the Department of Health and Social Security, but first of all read the relevant pamphlets, which are usually available at large post offices, so that you have a basic idea of what you are talking about, can ask the right questions, and recognise whether you are getting the right sort of answers instead of being lost in a fog of bureaucracy.

To sum up, if you decide to be an outworker, or homeworker, the basic contacts you should make are:

work sources
ACAS, the Low Pay Unit, or the Department of Employment (in cases of doubt over conditions and payment)
the Inspector of Taxes
the Department of Health and Social Security

The Business Man or Woman

If, however, you decide to set up your own business, either alone or as one of a group, or as an employer of outworkers, it is a very different matter. There are many people who will give help and advice, so many that the range and variety can be quite confusing.

Small Firms Service
To start with it's sensible to do your homework properly and to find out exactly what is involved in running a business, even a tiny one. Your first visit should probably be to the Small Firms Service. To contact this invaluable government-funded organisation all you need do is dial the telephone operator and ask for Freefone 2444. The Small Firms Service can put you in touch with all the people in your area who might be able to help you — local authority personnel, libraries, the chamber of commerce, and so on. If you need more than straightforward information — which is free — they will arrange for you to see a business counsellor who will be able to advise you personally. Three sessions with a counsellor come free of charge. For more you would be asked for a fee of £20 for up to a day's counselling. (These are the arrangements and fees of 1984 but may change.)

Enterprise Agencies

An alternative to the state-organised Small Firms Service is LENTA, the London Enterprise Agency. This is a private sector project specially designed to help and encourage the setting up and development of small firms. It holds both one-day courses (in 1984 the fee was £20) and four linked weekend courses covering every aspect of running a business. There is also follow-up counselling when problems occur.

As well as the London Enterprise Agency there are more than one hundred other enterprise agencies scattered throughout the United Kingdom from Aberdeen to Southampton, Great Yarmouth to Cardiff. To find out the one nearest you write to Business in the Community for their *Directory of Enterprise Agencies*. You'll find these addresses in Appendix 3.

Two of the organisations that the Small Firms Service and your local enterprise agency may put you in touch with are CoSIRA and the Crafts Council.

CoSIRA, the Council for Small Industries in Rural Areas, is, as the name implies, especially designed to help small, country-based firms, situated in places with a population of less than 12,000. It offers business training and financial advice, courses in a wide range of skills, and occasionally, grants for projects like the setting up of craft workshops and the development of studios from old farm buildings. As a rule small businesses are eligible for help provided that not more than twenty skilled people are employed. There is also an excellent CoSIRA *Handbook* in which craftspeople can have their names, addresses and details of their work listed county by county. Craft shops and galleries are also entered in a different section. Consequently, the shops know where to find their suppliers, the craftspeople know where to find their outlets, and the general public is given a complete picture of the crafts scene throughout the country

The Crafts Council is a government-funded body which aims to promote excellence in craft work. It has an invaluable information service with the following useful aids:

a list of craft fairs and markets where crafts can be sold

a register giving details of craftspeople, plus photographs of their work, so that retailers and the general public can see what is being produced
files dealing with suppliers of craft materials
a list of shops and galleries which include retail outlets
information about short and full-time craft courses throughout the country
information about regional arts associations and local craft guilds and societies, both of which are a useful source of contacts, support and encouragement
a reference section stocked with a wide range of craft magazines

The Crafts Council also publishes the excellent *Crafts* magazine which is not only a fund of up-to-date information about events, courses, suppliers, and so on, but also a beautifully produced and illustrated periodical which is sheer joy to read. The President of the American Craft Council recently wrote to the Editor of *Crafts*: 'I consider it the most beautiful and meaningful of the hundred art magazines I receive', and this high estimation is shared by many dedicated craftsmen and women.

In a few cases — though supply always exceeds demand — the council may be able to provide extra funding for new equipment, or to help with the setting up of a small workshop, under one of the schemes administered by the Grants and Loans Department, provided that the work reaches high levels of technical and aesthetic merit.

The council's marketing officer is available at the offices in Waterloo Place, London (see Appendix 3), to give advice on specific marketing problems, but it is necessary to make an appointment beforehand. Even for out-of-town craftspeople, a visit to the Crafts Council is a valuable exercise.

The Jobcentre

Before you go to the bank to organise money matters it is well worth calling in at the Jobcentre and asking for a leaflet called 'Guide to the Enterprise Allowance Scheme' for which you may be eligible. This allowance, which is an alternative to unemployment, or supplementary benefit, will pay you £40 a week (the rate for

1984) for a complete year to help you to get your business off the ground, and you may also get other benefits such as the Family Income Supplement, free school meals, rent and rate rebates.

The Bank Manager
By this time, having done your basic research and knowing precisely what is involved in running a small business, you should be fully prepared to go along and talk to a sympathetic and supportive bank manager and arrange to open a **business account,** which will be quite separate from any personal account you may have. A small business is best handled by a small local branch rather than a big city bank. Try to find one where every customer is known and treated as an individual with their own particular needs rather than just one number among the thousands on the computer.

The bank manager will discuss loan and overdraft facilities with you, and tell you about the various business services his bank offers. It is obviously better to have an overdraft instead of a loan if possible, but if you want to buy an expensive item like a sophisticated sewing- or knitting-machine, or to acquire an estate car or van, or lease premises, you may need to borrow.

Be prepared for the fact that the bank manager may ask some searching questions about your business plans — he will, after all, want to be quite sure that his money is safe in your keeping. Consequently, you need to have worked out some projected costings, and have an idea of your overheads and your profit margins, and so on, but the Small Firms Service can help you with this if necessary. Never misjudge or underestimate your financial requirements. False optimism is a common cause of business failure. If you have some other form of economic support — such as your husband's or wife's income — and plan to start in a small way, you won't need a lot of money to begin with, though you do need to take into account expenses such as buying large quantities of materials, advertising your service, and transporting the finished goods. If, however, you are trying to support yourself, and maybe a family too, you need to have enough money to live on for up to a year, as well as to pay the expenses of the business, before you can be sure that you will get a return on your outlay. Before you set foot inside the bank, work out whether you need to borrow, how much you need to borrow, how long it will take you to pay it back, and what security you have to offer. Perhaps an insurance policy will be acceptable. Don't give up if the first bank you approach refuses to co-operate. Find out why you have been turned down, rethink your case, then try another one.

In some cases, where an established business is potentially successful but needs extra cash, and a bank cannot offer support, it may be possible to get help under the Small Firms Loan Guarantee Scheme, through which the government provides your bank with a guarantee to cover 80 per cent of the amount borrowed. It is certainly worth asking your manager about it when you are ready to expand, and obtaining the leaflet 'Loan Guarantees for Small Businesses' from the Department of Industry.

If you are nervous about borrowing money, and can scrape together the capital you need from your own resources, you may be better off with an overdraft rather than a loan because the interest charges are likely to be lower. Do resist the temptation to borrow money from private finance organisations. Their rates of interest tend to be exorbitant.

The Accountant
The bank manager will probably suggest that you consider using the services of an accountant to help you keep your books in order and to prepare your accounts for the tax inspector. The best way to find a good accountant is by personal recommendation and again, go for one who is not too busy and successful to take a genuine personal interest in a small business venture. Unfortunately, accountants are expensive, so if you have a good head for figures and your operation is quite straightforward you may prefer to be responsible for the bulk of your own accounting. The Small Firms Service has guidelines to help you with this. However, it is worth having an initial counselling session with an accountant, just to get you going. One appointment will not cost a great deal of money,

and it's almost certain to be money well spent. When it comes to the end of the financial year and you have to prepare your books to present to the tax man you may decide to ask an accountant to draw up your balance sheet. He could save you money since he will know which of your expenses, such as advertising, postage, heating and lighting the rooms you use for business purposes, telephone costs, rent and rates, and running costs for your car can be set against tax. This is quite a complicated business, and the rules have a habit of changing from time to time, so professional expertise quite often pays for itself. Many business people claim that the only accountant worth employing is the one who can save his own fee from your tax bill!

It's worth asking your accountant about VAT, too. Though you need to have a turnover, not profits, in excess of £18,700 (1984) before it is compulsory to register, you can register below that figure, and this may have advantages in that you can claim back VAT that you have paid if, for instance, you are making goods such as children's clothes which are zero-rated. The VAT office produces a useful pamphlet, 'Should I Be Registered For VAT?' which will help to clarify the matter. You can find it by looking in the telephone directory where it is listed under 'Customs and Excise'.

There is a middle course between employing a fully qualified accountant and doing the job yourself, and that is to use a book-keeper or unqualified accountant who is experienced in preparing tax returns. If you ask around you will almost certainly have one recommended to you, but make sure that it is a recommendation you can trust because dishonesty, inefficiency, or a bungled attempt at tax evasion could be very damaging.

The Tax Inspector

When you begin your new enterprise you must tell your local inspector of taxes about your change in circumstances. To do this you should go to the tax office and pick up a leaflet 'IR.28 — Starting in Business' and fill in the form on the back. You will pay tax under Schedule D, which means that you can claim business expenses like those listed above against tax, and that you

will be charged tax once a year instead of on the PAYE system. If you have decided not to use an accountant the tax inspector will give you information about allowable expenses, but whether you have help or not you *must* keep careful daily records of your various expenses, as well as receipts, bills, invoices, cheque counterfoils, credit card vouchers, and so on. Chapter 8 deals in more detail with business organisation.

The Solicitor

It is reassuring, but not absolutely essential, to have at least one session with a solicitor, just to check that your proposed venture is within the law. If you want to run a business from your home, for instance, you will have to check whether there is anything in your deeds, leasehold or tenancy agreement which prevents it. If you need to extend or alter your property at all, to provide work-room or storage space perhaps, you will need to apply to the local authority for planning permission and for change of use. And if you get it, you will probably be faced with a higher rates bill for business usage. Another problem is that if your application for change of use is successful, and if you later come to sell your house which you originally bought as a domestic dwelling but has now become business premises, then a proportion of any profit you make will be subject to capital gains tax. A solicitor will be able to explain what precisely this will add up to in your particular circumstances.

It is possible to carry on a small business without having official permission. In many cases the hard-pressed local authority personnel would rather not know! But if you become very successful and busy, and neighbours begin to complain about the noise of machines, or about increased comings and goings of vans and cars, either bringing materials or taking away goods, then they could complain and stir up trouble. It is consequently a good idea to talk it over with neighbours *before* things start to happen. In that way they are much more likely to be tolerant, even positively encouraging and helpful, instead of feeling that you are taking liberties behind their backs.

A solicitor can advise on what formalities and

21

investigations are necessary, and help you to decide whether you should go-it-alone as a sole trader, or form a limited company, partnership, or co-operative. Briefly, the pros and cons are as follows:

Sole Trader
PROS
You are in charge, a free agent, and the business is entirely your affair and your personal 'baby'.

CONS
You have to shoulder the whole responsibility alone.
You may lose work if you are ill.
You may earn nothing while you are on holiday.
You may have only your own funds, resources, transport, storage space, equipment, and so on, to rely on.

Limited Company
PROS
If the business founders you are not personally responsible for its debts.

CONS
It will cost you £100+ to form.
There are a lot of regulations to observe, eg an annual audit and an annual return to the Registrar of Companies must be made.
Professional advice and assistance, which can be costly, is absolutely essential.

Partnership
PROS
You have someone with whom to share both the work and the worry, who will give you moral support and stimulate new ideas and initiatives. You can complement your own particular skills with others which you don't possess. You can draw on other people's equipment, transport and funds.

CONS
You are not in total control.
You have to take account of other people's wishes and ideas.
A *bad* partner makes life much more difficult than no partner at all, therefore it is vital to choose one with great care and have a trial period followed by a firm partnership agreement.

Co-operative
PROS
This is a highly democratic way of working and distributing profits and it can be very satisfying and pleasing.
There are bodies and organisations which positively foster, encourage and advise co-operatives.

CONS
You can founder if you are not in total agreement about your aims.
A great deal of time can be wasted in words instead of work unless the organisation is strong.

(For more information about co-operatives contact the Co-operative Development Agency and the Industrial Common Ownership Movement (ICOM) at the addresses given in Appendix 3.)

The Department of Health and Social Security
The matter of being in business on your own account, and therefore self-employed, will involve you in a visit to the DHSS to reorganise your National Insurance contribution. This has already been discussed in the section on outworkers at the beginning of the chapter and all that has been said there is relevant to the business craftsman or woman. The only difference is that the successful business venture could bring in more money than that acquired by an outworker, and if your earnings are over a specified limit — which changes from year to year — you may have to pay Class 4 contributions as well as Class 2. More details can be gained from leaflet 'NP.18 — Class 4 NI Contributions'.

The Insurance Broker
Personal insurance is important as well as National Insurance, so make contact with an insurance broker and ask his/her advice. Choose one small enough to be interested in you but not so small that he/she doesn't have a lot of insurance companies on the books. You may have to use your car for business purposes, picking up equipment or delivering stock, so your car insurance could change. You may also need insurance against losing your licence if you are totally reliant on being mobile. And it makes sense to insure the stock and equipment you keep on the premises, as well as your order books, contact books, patterns and designs. You should insure yourself against illness or injury and if you have a shop or work-room where

with compliments

The Dream Factory, Friday Street, Painswick, Gloucestershire GL6 6QJ. Tel: (0452) 812379

customers come to see you, you should be covered for public liability, too, just in case one of them has an accident for which you could be held responsible. Finally, if you employ staff, you will need employer's liability.

A broker will advise you about the various package deals offered by insurance companies and give you various quotes. Don't necessarily go for the cheapest which might have 'exclusion clauses' or 'excess amounts', because these could prevent you from being adequately recompensed if something nasty happens. Though insurance cover seems expensive if everything is going well, it will save you a fortune if everything goes wrong. An outbreak of fire or burst water pipes, a break-in, vandalism or theft, can cause devastation both physical and financial, and totally destroy an uninsured small business. When I ran a craft shop it was broken into three times in one month, and what the thieves didn't want they destroyed. Only my insurance broker's shrewd advice got me through that particular crisis.

The Printer
When you have organised the financial side of your new operation, worked out your business arrangements, taken legal advice, cleared your-

self as far as the tax office and the DHSS are concerned, and protected yourself with insurance, there's still one more major contact you need to make, and that's with a good printer.

The printer's skill will be necessary for:

some forms of advertising, eg handbills, car-stickers, posters, printed match-books, calendars, book-marks, personalised needlecases, etc
headed notepaper, business cards and compliment slips
invoices and bill-heads
personalised paper bags and carrier bags

It is very important to present yourself well right from the beginning and a small business which has the flair, and funds, to announce itself

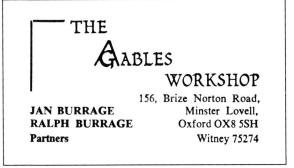

THE
ABLES
WORKSHOP
156, Brize Norton Road,
JAN BURRAGE   Minster Lovell,
RALPH BURRAGE   Oxford OX8 5SH
Partners   Witney 75274

on well-designed and printed stationery commands more respect and interest than one which relies on cheap lined writing pads and biro scribbles. Consequently, good-quality printing is an investment rather than a luxury.

Printers are, however, a variable breed. Some are fast, efficient, and reasonably priced. Others are hair-raisingly slow and inept. It's important to ask around in your area and to find out which ones can be trusted. Then ask to see examples of the work of several of them and collect a few estimates. A middle-sized printing firm with sufficient machinery and staff to be thoroughly reliable is usually the sort to go for. Neither a tiny business which has too much to do and not enough men or machinery, nor a huge concern which is used to dealing with accounts running into thousands of pounds, will be able to give you the sort of service you will be looking for. Find one you can trust to give you a fair deal and an attractive product, then stick with it — it will be worth its weight in gold.

This period in the starting up of a business, when you are learning your trade, finding your contacts, thinking out your strategy and laying your plans, can be great fun and a very exciting time, but it will probably last a month or two. If possible, you should use these months to their maximum benefit by discovering where the other needlecraft exponents are to be found in your part of the country. The CoSIRA *Handbook* will be of great help in tracking them down. If you can make contact with them you might have the opportunity to exchange ideas, discover new techniques, methods and sources of supply, and stimulate your creative imagination. You should *not*, of course, be wandering about stealing other people's best designs or trying to muscle in on their patch and their customers. But the craft world can be a warm, supportive community where workers encourage each other and genuinely enjoy each others' talents and achievements. It's not a place of cut-throat competition but one of shared endeavour — which makes it a particularly pleasant place to be.

4 Finding Help or Going-It-Alone

Once you have decided that you want to make money from your craft, the next major decision is whether you will work alone or in a group, whether you will be employed or employ others, whether you will use outworkers or form a partnership, and so on. The various possibilities are extensive.

Outworking

This has been an established cottage industry for hundreds of years. An outworker is, by definition, a person over 18 who works on his/her own premises, is provided with work, and returns the completed articles to the provider. There are more than 150,000 of them in the United Kingdom. As explained in the previous chapter, they pay their own tax and National Insurance, and some of them, including those involved in buttonmaking, toymaking and the manufacture of women's light clothing, have their earnings regulated by the Wages Council, though this does not prevent their wages from being very low. However, if you

prefer to be organised rather than do the organising you will perhaps not mind that too much, for there are advantages. Many outworking craftspeople, especially knitters, would rather work for nothing than not work at all, and *anything* they get paid for their craft is looked upon as a bonus. This is, nevertheless, no excuse for exploitation, and there are moves afoot to safeguard people who work from home in this country. To start with, the British Code of Advertising Practice insists that:

> advertisements should make it clear whether the outworker will be charged for machinery and materials supplied for use
> advertisements should give an adequate description of the scheme, and the reward to be expected
> the conditions under which goods made by the outworker will be bought by the advertiser should be clearly stated

It is *not* wise to send money to an advertiser under the impression that this will enable you to make money. Nor should you imagine that laying out capital on an expensive machine is necessarily a good investment and that you will rapidly recover your costs — there is no guarantee of this. A reputable employer should provide the machine. He or she should also give you some idea of how much work there will be and what delivery and collection arrangements have been made. *Never* agree to pay for travel, transport and postage out of your own pocket. Another problem that occasionally occurs is that you may be required to provide a lot of storage space for materials — and these could include allergic or inflammable materials which are not only unpleasant to have in the house but could affect the house and contents insurance as well as the health and safety of the occupants. Finally, you should investigate the conditions under which things that you make could be rejected by an employer — it occasionally happens that a whole batch of goods can be turned down because there is a small flaw in one item, and that adds up to a great deal of wasted time, money and effort.

If you are in any doubt about the sort of deal offered in an advertisement there will be advisers at the Citizens' Advice Bureau who will help you to discover whether there are pitfalls, and remember that the Low Pay Unit (see Appendix 3) acts as a kind of watchdog over the experiences and treatment of homeworkers.

Employing Outworkers

It may be that you would prefer to be in business on your own account and either do everything yourself or use outworkers to help you. Find them through your local grapevine and contacts, or by advertising in your local paper or corner shop. It's usually better to have people in the neighbourhood rather than scattered about the country and having to rely upon the post office and telephone services to get things organised. The use of a team of outworkers can give very good results provided that you have skilled reliable people and a happy working relationship with them. It is always worth giving them a sample job to do first of all, to make sure that their standards are high enough, and then to use them for a trial period to make sure that they can consistently do the work on time and

maintain the quality of their output.

It is difficult to set hourly or piece-work rates because two factors have to be taken into account which may be incompatible:

1 The outworker must not be paid so much that the eventual cost of the goods becomes too high to be competitive.
2 The outworker must not be paid so little that either she or he becomes resentful and produces shoddy work, or you find that you are breaking the law by paying less than the minimum legal wage. You can check up on this by contacting the Low Pay Unit.

It is absolutely vital to do your costings very carefully — as outlined in Chapter 8 — but you should also treat people justly and give them a fair return for their labour, even if, in desperation, they would do it for less. At the end of your financial year you should give each of your workers a note of how much she or he has earned as well as filing away a copy for your accountant to show the tax man.

One disadvantage of employing outworkers can be that you yourself become an administrator rather than a craftsperson and spend your life car-bound, delivering and collecting. One of the ways to avoid this is to use people who live near you, and near each other, and to have a regular weekly run sufficiently planned in advance to manage all the fetching and carrying in one session, rather than to have to make repeated trips. This makes sense as far as petrol costs and car wear-and-tear are concerned, as well as the value of your time. Alternatively, you can use one of the outworkers as an organiser, showing her exactly what you want, handing over the materials, and letting her sort out the practical side of the operation while you get on with the creative side, designing, developing ideas, making patterns, co-ordinating colours, choosing and matching fabrics, cutting, shaping, and so on.

From a legal point of view your business arrangement with your outworkers is critical and needs to be carefully planned. At present they are classed as casual labour, responsible for their own insurance and tax. Many of them prefer this arrangement though there is a move to in-state them as employees, and the law could change within the foreseeable future. Already, the Factories Act lays down that employers should register outworkers with the local authority, but only a tiny number do, and such a provision is almost impossible to enforce. Being a casual labourer as opposed to being a legal employee means that if there is no work available an outworker can suddenly find herself without an income and also without unemployment benefit or redundancy payment, even if she has been working for a large company. In these circumstances she can appeal, with the help of the Citizens' Advice Bureau, or a Legal Advice Centre, and discover that in the eyes of the law her work circumstances add up to the fact that she has in reality, been 'employed' and can be reclassified. There have been cases of this kind recently and they have not been good news for the employer who, in all innocence, had not paid employer's NI contributions or issued the required warnings of termination of employment. If it goes to an Industrial Tribunal the employer may find it necessary either to reinstate the outworker, or to pay redundancy money, as well as making back payments of NI contributions, and obviously this can be a very costly business.

The way to avoid this is to make sure that your outworkers are working properly on a freelance basis with self-employed status, paying their own tax and National Insurance, and thus protecting themselves through DHSS benefits from hardship through illness or lack of work. If they earn less than £32.50 a week (as of April 1983) they are not liable for NI contributions anyway, and if they work for you for less than sixteen hours a week there is no official contract of employment between you.

Employing Staff

When a business is established and thriving, especially when it is functioning from business premises rather than a home base, it may become necessary to employ staff, but it is better not to rush into this prematurely in a first fine flush of optimism. There are difficulties — mainly due to the legislation embodied in the Employment Protection Act. The first is the

hidden expenses. On top of his/her wage an employee must have holiday pay and employer's National Insurance contributions. If a business has to close down or reduce its work force and the employee is made redundant, then if he or she has been employed for a minimum of two years he or she will be entitled to redundancy pay, based on length of service and salary scale, and half of this will be payable by you.

The second is the complication of getting rid of staff who have worked for you for a minimum of 52 weeks — or 104 weeks in the case of a new business. Fair grounds for terminating employment are misconduct, incompetence or redundancy, but these have to be proved and there is a web of written warnings and reasons to be worked through.

If a dismissed employee feels that you have been unfair you may find yourself taken before an Industrial Tribunal, and if you lose your case it can be a very expensive business. It should not be contemplated without legal advice.

Linked to this is the complication of maternity leave. If a full-time employee who has been on your staff for a minimum of 2 years works until 11 weeks before giving birth, she is legally allowed to take off 40 weeks, and then return to work (if you have a staff of 6 or more), and during this time you must keep her job open for her. While she is absent you may have to substitute another worker in her place but you must be very careful to spell out *in writing* right from the beginning that this is only a temporary appointment and give notice when it is coming to an end, otherwise the replacement worker will be able to sue you for unfair dismissal.

Finally, there are the complications of making sure that you conform with health and safety at work requirements, and of handling the paper work which is caused by your having to be responsible for employees' Pay-As-You-Earn arrangements and being accountable for them to the tax office.

So, think twice about employing people as opposed to using freelance, self-employed workers, and before you take this step call in at your local Department of Industry and get advice plus the explanatory pamphlet, 'Employing People', to help you understand all that is involved. In any event, you should apply to the local authority for planning permission if you want to employ anyone to work in your home. If permission is refused — and it might be because they don't like people turning their homes into workshops — you have a right to appeal. Should you get confused in this labyrinth, the Jobcentre or Small Firms Service will be able to advise you as to which department to contact about what.

After all this you may decide that you would like to work with people who will share your work-load and responsibilities but that neither outworkers nor employees fit the bill. If this is the case you need to think about the relative merits of setting up a co-operative or forming a partnership.

Setting Up a Co-operative

Worker-co-operatives are becoming an increasingly popular form of organising small business ventures. In 1971 there were less than a dozen in the United Kingdom. Today, there are over 800, employing approximately 8,000 people, and 5 or 6 new ones are being formed every week.

In the most general of terms, a co-operative is an organisation which is both owned and controlled by those who work in it, on a completely democratic basis of one person, one vote. Only people actively involved in it have a right to be members and all those people have a right to be members. Money invested in the enterprise does not give any right of control, so there is no such thing as a 'sleeping partner' and the members do not have any financial liability in the event of debt or bankruptcy.

The primary advantage of working in a co-operative is that it can be a very satisfying way of sharing the pleasures, and the worries, of work with other people who are all equally committed to the enterprise. It is, in fact, a way of life rather than simply a pattern of work.

The primary disadvantage is that since there is no leader, and decisions are made by the group, the decision-making process can be a very long and tedious one. All the co-operatives I interviewed spent hours talking. One wrote to me:

We'll have to discuss whether we want to be in your book, and whether we want to have a conversation with you, or whether we would rather write about ourselves. I expect we'll have a meeting next week to talk about whether we want to talk to you, and then we'll let you know.

This is typical of co-operative procedure. For those who like speed and action and are used to more authoritarian and decisive ways of working it can prove very frustrating.

Whether you would function well in a co-operative depends largely upon your temperament and experience, but at least the possibility is worth investigating. It is an interesting statistic, and an encouraging one, that co-operatives are far less prone to business failure than conventionally structured set-ups. This is probably due to the members' shared commitment to the ideal of equal ownership and control. It is also true that as a result of the women's movement, many women are rebelling against the authoritative hierarchical structures of 'bosses and workers' that they feel men have created, and prefer to work in looser structures without leaders.

To find out more write to both the Co-operative Development Agency and the Industrial Common Ownership Movement, both of which are listed in Appendix 3. The Co-operative Development Agency is an advisory body set up by parliament. It has no funds to invest but it can give general guidance and suggest sources of both financial assistance and practical support. As well as working on a national level there are many local co-operative development agencies throughout the country, and several local authorities have co-operative development officers. The CDA will provide lists of useful addresses, useful reading material, and useful videotapes, and they have their own publications, including a valuable information pack *How To Set Up a Worker Co-operative*, priced at £2.50. This contains advice about co-operative organisation, business planning, legal structures, raising finance, finding premises, and lists of support organisations and resource material.

ICOM also publishes several books including *How To Form an Industrial Co-operative* which is a kit describing the processes to be gone through, and including the necessary registration forms as well as a set of model rules. This is free to associate members of ICOM when they pay their first annual subscription, or it can be bought by non-members for £10.50.

Forming a Partnership

Partnerships can be much more flexible than co-operatives, but they have the huge disadvantage that all the partners are equally financially liable in the case of debt, even though that debt may have been incurred by just one partner without the others having been involved or even having any knowledge of it.

Simply going into business with at least one other person creates a partnership in law but it is wise to make up a carefully considered partnership agreement, spelling out each individual's role and responsibilities. It may be that some partners put in more money than work, or vice versa. It may be that some have more voting power than others. It may be that some have different skills — for instance, a three-fold partnership could be evolved containing a business/legal/financial organiser, a sales person and a crafts person. Alternatively, it could contain craftspeople whose skills complement each other and who share the administrative work.

One partnership group I met contained a patchwork maker, a dressmaker, a knitwear specialist, a cushion maker, a children's clothes maker, and a woodworker, and they had a financial adviser who was not a partner. They sold from a market stall and their organisation was simple and practical. Financially, the craftsmen paid for their own material and equipment, priced their own goods, and kept 90 per cent of what they took. The other 10 per cent went into a kitty which paid their expenses, the rent for their market stall, their stationery and polythene bags. Any extra profits were shared out equally. Other matters were controlled by a membership charter which covered the process to be gone through when any newcomer joined the group, a roster which determined who was serving on the stall and when, and a monthly meeting to discuss policy and progress.

Your solicitor will help with the business of drawing up a partnership agreement to suit your particular needs and this should include such matters as:

> individual jobs and responsibilities
> decision-making rights
> investment of money and of time
> division of profits
> management during the illness or absence of a partner
> admitting new partners
> procedure if one partner leaves
> disposing of assets if the partnership is dissolved, etc

In my experience, the most important factor in any partnership or co-operative arrangement is that the people involved are compatible and enjoy working together. Nothing destroys the happiness and satisfaction of an enterprise more than personal irritations and constant disagreements, so choose your fellow-workers with care and look for people who are sensible and energetic, cheerful and efficient, and totally reliable, and who share your own commitment and pleasure.

One problem which affects many craftspeople is that they enjoy *making* things, but they don't enjoy *selling* them. In fact, many of the marvellously skilled craftsmen and women whom I interviewed confessed that they could hardly believe that the things they made were good enough for people actually to want to spend money on! This humility can make life very difficult because unless you are able to sell with sufficient confidence and enthusiasm you won't find sufficient buyers — few will find the time to beat a path to your door in the first instance.

Using an Agent

One solution to the problem — apart from having a partner who is responsible for the selling side of the business — is to appoint an agent. This can work extremely well provided that you choose the right agent. You can find them advertising their services in *Crafts* magazine, or you can take the initiative and advertise yourself, along the following lines:

Agent required, East Anglia. Preferably experienced in high-quality, hand-made, patchwork and quilted garments. Details — Patchy Poll, 27 Harbour Lane, Great Yarmouth.

The right agent will:

be knowledgeable and enthusiastic about your particular craft
have high standards for his/her clients so that there is no chance of your goods being sold alongside badly made rubbish
be able to prove to your satisfaction that he/she has a good sales record and a comprehensive list of retail outlets
take a stand at at least one trade exhibition each year
be able to produce good references which you *must* check if you are to avoid being duped by a clever confidence-trickster. (Remember that you are going to trust this person with your goods and your reputation)

An agent will probably ask only for a commission on what is sold, but there may also be a small retainer fee to cover initial expenses. Make sure that you have your financial agreement *in writing* from the beginning, to avoid arguments about who gets what after your crafts have been sold.

Being an Agent

You may, of course, enjoy selling so much yourself that you are particularly happy to get away from your workbench occasionally to meet your customers. It is obviously very useful to see for yourself how they respond to what you make, and to listen very carefully to what they say, the brick-bats as well as the bouquets. In this way you can find out not only what is popular but *why*, and it will help you with future designing and colour co-ordination and the development of new lines. Often the craftsperson working in isolation becomes out of touch with the customers he/she is trying to please. This is not only bad for business, it can also mean missing out on the lovely experience of seeing the pleasure and admiration with which your work is greeted.

If you find marketing fun, and are good at it, you might like to act as an agent for one or more crafts colleagues with complementary products, selling a varied range instead of just your own things. This need not make your overheads and transport costs any higher and you will have the financial bonus of commission to add to your earnings. When I ran my craft shop I often preferred to look at more than one range of goods at a sitting because it saved my time and made it more likely that I would find something I wanted to buy. If you can walk into a baby shop and produce not only your own cot quilts but also soft toys, baby clothes and christening robes the buyer will find you a very useful contact, just as a kitchen shop would be happy to look at a variety of pinafores, oven-gloves, tablecloths and napkins, padded cosies, and so on. Alternatively, you could stick to only one line but have such a variety within it that everyone would find something that looks right and is in the right price range. Supposing you are a knitter of fabulous sweaters. It could make sense to gather around you a group of other talented knitters, all specialists in different styles and techniques, and sell their work along with your own on a commission basis.

There are innumerable ways of organising your working life if you want to make money from your craft. The one that suits you best will depend upon many factors:

your temperament
your financial standing and aims
the outlets and facilities of the place where you live
the hours that you can give to your craft
the craft itself

But there is almost certainly one of them that will suit you, whatever your circumstances.

5 Equipment

When you are beginning to establish yourself as a professional craftsperson you do not necessarily need to invest a large amount of money in machinery. Very often the basic tools of the trade are simply **needles.** A hand-knitter is fortunate in that she needs little more than a few pairs of knitting needles and a sewing-up needle to get her started. In fact, she may never need much more than that because there is a great demand for hand-knitting as opposed to machine-knitting and big firms like Patons will not accept machine-knitted garments for their demonstration models. Similarly, many types of embroidery or needlepoint need only the right sort of needles, and crochet needs little more than a crochet hook. Macramé work requires even less since it is based on knotting rather than stitching. Though most macramé workers use a board on to which to pin their foundation threads it is possible to use the legs of an up-turned chair, or clamps fixed on either side of a table top, or a variety of other sorts of homespun bases.

Nevertheless, if you are aiming for swift and elegant results, and if you want to be paid a reasonable hourly rate for your labour, sooner or later you will probably find it necessary to invest in some sort of machinery. None of the dressmakers I spoke to did all their work by hand — they all used a sewing-machine of some sort, but it was surprising how often it was a sturdy old machine without the elaborations and refinements found on current models. The following table shows at a glance the sort of equipment required for the range of needlecrafts by which people earn money. It can be acquired gradually as you begin to build up a little profit from early sales, or the bank may be persuaded to give you a loan for capital investment if you can persuade the manager that it is going to increase your profitability.

Appliqué embroidery: needles and/or swing-needle sewing-machine.
Canvaswork (needlepoint): needles; embroidery frame.
Crochet: crochet hook.
Dressmaking and alterations: sewing-machine with full range of attachments; overlocker;

tailor's dummy; hanging rail.

Embroidery — goods and garments: needles; embroidery frame and/or sewing-machine with attachments.

Lacemaking: lace pillow; bobbins.

Macramé: macramé board; crochet hook (optional).

Making handbags: sewing-machine(s) — preferably one domestic and one heavy duty for a full range of fabrics; overlocker.

Making (and/or trimming) hats: needles, sewing-machine; hat blocks; steaming kettle (*without* automatic cut-out); egg iron for shaping; pliers.

Making knitwear and knitted goods: knitting-needles and/or knitting-machine; pressing-machine; stretching frame (optional).

Making silk flowers: needles and/or sewing-machine.

Making soft-furnishings: heavy-duty sewing-machine with piping foot.

Making soft lampshades: sewing-machine; wire frames.

Making soft leather goods: strong needles and/or heavy-duty sewing-machine with attachments; sharp craft knife; cutting board.

Making soft shoes: heavy-duty sewing-machine; sharp craft knife; cutting board.

Making soft toys: needles and/or sewing-machine with zig-zag; overlocker (optional).

Patchwork and quilting: sewing needles and/or sewing-machine; quilting frame (optional); plastic or metal templates (optional).

Ribbon weaving: needles; board.

It is also vital to possess, in most cases, the following:

excellent large scissors and sometimes small ones, too
an accurate measure — often a ruler is better than a tape since it neither stretches nor frays
a good steam iron, or, for knitters, an electric pressing-machine
one or two large tables or work benches
an ironing-board, perhaps with sleeve attachment
a comfortable chair, at the right height and providing adequate back support
a lot of storage space, small drawers, large drawers, cupboards and shelves, to hold materials of all

kinds, from tiny packets of pins to huge bolts of fabric
good light, both general and concentrated
adequate heating — cold is counter-productive if your work is sedentary.

Finally, for business efficiency, it is is good to have:

some sort of filing system for invoices, receipts, letters, brochures
a typewriter for your business correspondence, and — when you can afford it —
a small photocopier. This will enable you to keep duplicates of important documents and photocopy good design ideas and illustrations, as well as useful details, names, addresses, and so on, from books and magazines.

It should be obvious by now that if you are really intending to take yourself seriously you need a room of your own. This may be a spare bedroom, which is the most usual starting-off place for the freelance home-based worker. Alternatively, the family might be happy to let you have the dining-room while the living-room or kitchen acquires a dining area. Other ways of finding an extra room are to adapt a loft or basement cellar, to acquire a capacious garden shed, making sure that it is weather-proof and well insulated, or to build on some form of extension — for which, of course, you'll have to apply for planning permission.

All this adds up to a counsel for perfection to be aimed at eventually. At the beginning you will probably have to make do with what you've got, but that's no bad thing. I met many a superb craftswoman who had begun with her mother's cast-off treadle-machine which was often much older than she was, and her 'workshop' had been a corner of the kitchen table. Nevertheless, it is worthwhile organising some space for yourself, and investing in suitable new or second-hand machinery, either for knitting or sewing, as soon as you can if your craft would benefit by it. The

Plate 1 Handmade patchwork items from Wendy Burton, Wendy Beatrix Designs: 'Tall Pine Trees' patchwork wall hanging; matching Gretel dresses; 'Floral Triangle' jacket and 'Bumble' waistcoat

sort of questions you should ask yourself before you buy are:

has it the range of attachments I need to do all the jobs I want to do, and do I feel thoroughly competent to use them?

is the instruction book simple to follow or totally unintelligible?

am I paying a lot for gadgets I don't want and won't use?

can I get the machine regularly serviced and quickly repaired if necessary?

does it make so much noise that other people in the house are going to feel miserable?

has it been recommended by friends, by craft magazines, or by a magazine such as *Which?*, and, most important,

do I feel really happy and confident about it?

Shop around very carefully before you make your choice. Ask for advice, comparative information, brochures and demonstrations, and, if a shop cannot be bothered to take the time and trouble to answer your questions, go elsewhere. When you decide upon your machine don't buy it until you are absolutely sure that you know exactly how it works. There are many knitters' clubs throughout the country and they are a fund of information. You could try writing to the Worldwide Machine Knitters' Club at the address given in Appendix 3. Enclose a stamped addressed envelope and ask for their advice. Alternatively, rummage in the library for *The Batsford Book of Hand and Machine Knitting* by Tessa Lorant or *A Resource Book for Machine Knitters* by Kathleen Kinder, both of which are extremely helpful. Kathleen Kinder will answer personal queries from The Dalesknit Centre (see address in Appendix 6).

Knitmaster machines were top of the pops among the knitters I spoke to, but recently a new hand-knitting frame machine came on to the market and is causing a minor revolution in the knitting world. It is called a Bond, knits a wide range of hand-knit yarns including mohair, bouclé, chunky, cotton, and ribbon, as well as double-knit, Aran and brushed 4-ply, and gives a real hand-knit look and quality to the finished

Plate 2   A beautiful wedding dress from Jo Palmer, The Dream Factory (Keith Davies)

garment. It is so simple that total beginners can teach themselves to use it in just a few hours from the instruction books that are all in pictures. A colour book of patterns comes with the machine, too. To me its main attractions are that it is easy to adapt hand-knit patterns to the machine, and since hand-knit stitches are easily transferred to the Bond it is also possible to combine machine-knitting and hand-knitting. You just whizz through the boring bits, then do the interesting bits by hand if you prefer.

The Bond weighs only 4lb (1.8kg) and can be used on any table. It takes a couple of minutes to set up, cast on and start knitting, and can be packed away in seconds. It needs no maintenance or oiling since it has no moving parts, levers, dials, buttons or punch cards, and — best of all — it costs about half as much as its nearest Japanese competitor. Its inventor won *The Observer* Innovations for Industry award in 1981, and it is the first knitting-machine ever to carry the Design Centre label.

Bond Knitting Systems run regular Creative Knitting courses in London, given by professional knitwear designers. Anyone interested in them, or the machine, should write to them at:

Unit 21
Bridge Street Mill
Bridge Street
Witney
Oxford OX8 6YH

For sewing-machines and overlockers, the best way to find out what the various models can do is to have them demonstrated either at specialist shops, like Singer, or in big department stores which carry a lot of machines made by many manufacturers throughout the world, so that you can make comparisons. Specialist needlecraft magazines often advertise, test and comment on new machines on the market, and browsing through one or two of them should help you to clarify your ideas.

Finally, if you have chosen carefully and wisely, and if you are prepared to cherish your machine, look after it, keep it clean and well maintained, then use it regularly and learn to look upon it as a friend and ally, it will repay you with many years of useful service.

6 Getting Started and Getting Known

When you have investigated and organised the legal and financial aspects of your business venture, have decided whether to work on your own or as one of a group of some sort or another, and have made sure that your skills, and your equipment and work space are in good order, then the time has come to take the next step — to get your idea off the ground and find your customers.

The first priority should be to decide whether you are going to trade under your own name, or part of it, or to make up a name for your business. Some people are quite happy with what they are called and there's nothing at all wrong with 'Penny Price, Toymaker' or 'Lindy Wright Knits'. One or two craftsmen like to make a new coinage from their own name and the thing that they make, so the toymaker, Rusty Grimmond, has become 'Rustoys', and Jane Playford, with her lacemaking and needlecraft equipment business, calls herself 'Jane's Pincushion'. But you may want to differentiate between your personal identity and your professional persona and choose something quite new. Names should be like signature tunes. They need to be attractive, catchy and memorable but they should also give some indication or flavour of the type of craft with which they are linked. In other words, the style or essence of the title should both attract attention and complement the product. I came across many pretty, suitable and clever names while I was contacting craftsmen. Some were succinctly descriptive, like 'Carpet Bags'. Some of them had a rhythmic and alliterative lilt, like 'Ragged Robin', 'Penny Plain' and 'Klassy Kits'. Some used clever rhymes, like 'Suzy Q'. Some indicated quite subtly what they were aiming at — 'Shimmer' for pure silk lingerie; 'Sleepwalkers' for nightdresses and sleepwear; 'Over the Rainbow' for multicoloured sweaters; 'The Dream Factory' for clothes to make your loveliest dreams come true. And then there were the funny, witty ones — 'Drafties', for a firm that sells daft draught excluders, 'Swanky Modes' for a group of bright young fashion designers, and 'Woolly Bloomers' for a husband and wife team that makes knitted pot plants. They could equally well have chosen 'Potty Plants'!

It is important, however, to keep within the law when choosing a name. It is no longer necessary to register it with the Registrar of Business Names, but it is required, since the Companies Act of 1981, that if you are working as a sole trader or as a partnership under a name other than your own you must display your name(s) and business address on all your stationery — letterheads, order forms, receipts, invoices, and so on. You also have a statutory duty to display your name and address in the place from which you conduct your business, and to give your name and address if required to both customers and suppliers. So it's fine to head your letters with 'Toys for Tots', 'Woolly Pullies' or 'Sweet Dreams' as long as, somewhere on the page, you add 'Jane Smith, 23 The Causeway, Bridlington', or whatever.

The legislation covering limited companies is more complicated. Names must be properly registered with the Registrar of Companies at Companies Registration Office, and this should be done through an accountant or solicitor.

It is sad but true that even if you have thought up an original and appropriate name for yourself and it seems exclusively yours you cannot prevent anyone else from using it. Names are not copyright. The only way to gain sole rights to a name is to form a limited company, and in this case you must check, first of all, with the Companies Registration Office to make sure that no one else is using it.

As soon as you have decided on a name you can go along to your printer and order your business stationery. It may be that you have designed a personal logo to give individual and visual distinction to your cards and letterheads, and this will become your trademark. A logo is a very good idea since it fulfils several functions without the need for words. It attracts the eye; engages the attention; creates an impression, and, if it is good, imprints itself upon the memory, and all of these are, of course, an important part of advertising technique. Nevertheless, it is vital to talk it over with your printer first of all because it may make your stationery bills more expensive.

Your first use for your name (and logo) will probably be for letterheads like some of those shown here. Headed notepaper gives an impression of efficient business organisation and undoubtedly inspires more confidence than hand-written letters. The other forms of printed material you may find useful are:

> business cards and 'with compliments' slips which you can give to customers and potential customers; handbills, which, if they are carefully planned and attractively designed, can show a good representative sample of your work

If you are setting up an ambitious business project from scratch, as opposed to starting small and growing gradually, you may also find

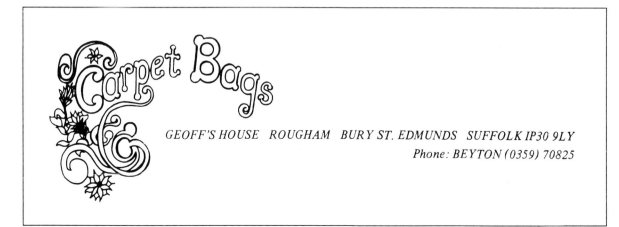

GEOFF'S HOUSE   ROUGHAM   BURY ST. EDMUNDS   SUFFOLK IP30 9LY
Phone: BEYTON (0359) 70825

it useful to invest in small posters and car-stickers, and give-away advertising goods such as book-marks, book-matches, or little card needlecases like those some big hotels now provide for their guests.

All of these things imprint your name and the goods you make in a very useful way provided that they are smart and attractive, and give information about *who* you are, *where* you are, and *what* you create.

Finally, as soon as you can afford it, it's good to have your own personalised paper or polythene bags and/or carrier bags in which customers can carry away their purchases, and to have specially made labels which are either sewn into or on to what you have made so that it is a constant reminder of your skill to whoever should see it. (Don't make the mistake of writing the price on the ticket that carries details about your business if it is the sort of thing that will be given away as a gift — otherwise the buyer will have to remove it before the receiver knows who made it.) Bags, carriers and labels may seem to have more to do with presentation than getting known, and are consequently covered in Chapter 9, but the fact remains that they are also an invaluable form of advertising since they carry your name far and wide.

Once you have acquired your advertising and promotional materials the next step is to make sure that that they reach the potential customers you hope to attract. The first, cheapest and most obvious place to put one of your cards or hand-bills is in your corner shop or post office window, or on the advertising board of your nearest supermarket. Many newsagents will also slip a handbill inside their newspapers and charge very little for this service, or you can pop advertising material through letter-boxes your-self, with a little bit of help from friends and family, or pay someone else to do the legwork for you. It depends upon how much time and energy you possess or how much money you need to save.

Alternatively, you can place an advertisement in your local paper or free advertising paper. These are some from my own local advertiser which may give you ideas.

> Beautiful beading and sequin work carried out on all lace garments. Wedding dresses a speciality. Please reply to Box XX

> Fashion clothes exclusively designed and made to fit you. Also interior design, decorating and soft furnishing service. Tel. 123 456

> Curtains and loose covers. I call, measure and fit. Select the material in your own home. Tel: 654 321

> Experienced dressmaker will make any item of clo-thing, also alterations. Please reply: Box YY

Do make sure that your advertisement is accurate. If you say your goods are washable and they don't wash; if you claim that they are pure wool and they are wool and synthetic fibre; if you say they are not inflammable and they go up like a torch; if, in fact, your description is mis-leading in any way at all, then you could be in trouble as a result of the Trades Descriptions Act.

Local papers — and, indeed, national ones — are often avid for stories and you may well be able to talk the features editor or chief reporter into doing a little feature about you, provided that your venture is newsworthy. To catch journalistic attention you do need to have some-

thing different to offer. If you are simply making up other people's material into well-made but conventional garments, or producing a range of bunnies and teddies just like a thousand other bunnies and teddies, your activities are not likely to command much attention. If, however, you are a young designer creating zany, outrageous clothes the like of which have never been seen before; if you are a toymaker specialising in giant reptiles, monsters and space creatures instead of cuddly little animals; if you make children's sweaters that squeak, cushions that look like ham sandwiches and icecream cones, knitted houseplants, Dracula cloaks — then you are making news. Similarly, if there's a human interest story lurking behind your business operation a reporter may find this a line worth following up. I have read about a highly success-ful industrialist who left the bright lights of London for the pale sands of Barra to create an island cottage industry with his own group of knitters. I have been intrigued by a talented potter who took a year off from her wheel to learn about rearing Jacob's sheep, only to find herself at the centre of a thriving spinning and weaving concern. And Jane Playford, the lacemaker, admitted in her interview (p70) that her turnover doubled as soon as she became the wife of a Falklands hero instead of merely a local craftswoman. All these people made the news, and increased their business, because there was something about their lives that was guaranteed to rouse interest.

What is true of the papers is also true of radio, especially local radio, and regional television. So, if you've got a good story to tell, try and persuade the media to let you tell it. It's the best possible form of publicity.

The national dailies, Sunday papers and glossy magazines pose more of a problem than local papers simply because there is so much more newsworthy material available to them to choose from. Nevertheless, some of them regu-larly carry details about craft work and interest-ing money-making ventures and they *are* assail-able, if you have the confidence to approach them. Many of the craftspeople interviewed in Chapter 10 had been featured on the pages of the *Daily Telegraph, The Times, The Guardian,*

Woman's Realm, Family Circle, Woman's Own, Vogue, Popular Crafts, and so on, usually as a result of sending in some information, preferably illustrated, about who they were and what they did. These are all effective publications in which to place an advertisement, too, though they are very expensive. The trouble is, they can create a demand which is very difficult to fill without large resources and a good team of workers behind you. And they can involve you in a marathon of posting and packaging which can strain your budget and your available time. Consequently, it is very important before you either advertise in a mass readership paper or allow them to carry a story about you to make sure that you are prepared to cope with the orders that may flood in as a result. (On the other hand you must also be prepared for the fact that your advertisement or news story might produce nothing at all except massive apathy — which could be even more upsetting!)

If you are sufficiently geared up to sell on a large scale, look at the newspapers very carefully, and especially at their advertisement columns, before you decide which is right for you and which is most likely to bring your product to the attention of the sort of people who would be attracted by it. It is probable that an expensive quality item will sell better through an expensive quality newspaper. Certainly, if you like the things that you see advertised in a specific publication it seems reasonable to expect that other readers will admire the sort of goods that you would advertise there. Make sure that your advertisement uses its space to utmost eye-catching advantage, perhaps by adding visual details to words.

If you hope to get coverage in the feature pages, or to arouse some interest on radio or television, it is wise to create your own press release with photographs and/or illustrations as well as information about yourself, your product and your background, told briefly but as interestingly as possible, and to send this to the editor of the relevant section of the paper or magazine or to the producer of the most likely radio or TV programme. To find the right target you must do your homework properly — read, look, listen and find out where and when craft enterprises are most likely to be covered, whether they occur in the women's pages, the consumer columns, the business supplements, and so on. Keep your information sheet bright, attractive, lively and concise. Make sure that you have put on your name and telephone number, and with luck it will elicit some response. It may be printed almost as it stands, or in a condensed version, or it might trigger off a phone call and perhaps an interview, too. This may *seem* unduly optimistic but it isn't. The media are always on the look-out for material, as Wendy Burton emphasises in her interview on p99. Her group, 'Ashdown Artisans', took great pains with their publicity, and I was the journalist approached by *Living* magazine and asked to go and interview them as a result of their initiative.

Here are three stories from three very different magazines, but all concerned with small-scale craft ventures. This is the sort of publicity you could get for your own if you have a good interesting product and know how to promote it. They were picked out at random from:

A   *Family Circle* (January 1984)
B   *Home & Freezer Digest* (July 1984)
C   *Company* (June 1983)

A   Knitted to Fit

Big girls are warned off woollies from the very moment they assume those bonus pounds that more ordinary mortals don't have. So when someone offers them knits designed to suit their size — and made to measure, to boot — they respond, readily.

Anne Kent started her business knitting for stock sizes. Now those that keep her busiest at her machine are size 16s and over. Her average order is for a 40in bust but she does up to 50 (that's as far as the machine can go!).

'If you make skirts fluid and knit them sideways,' explains Anne, 'they're as slimming as ones in other materials and won't "sit out". Anyway, I study the measurements I'm sent and balance top half and lower half by adjusting jacket or sweater lengths to avoid a stumpy effect.'

FC's ambassador for size 16s and over, layout artist Amanda Rayner, chose this top and skirt from Anne's styles. You can see the full range if you send an sae, 9in by 7½in, to Anne Kent, 125 Farley Road, South Croydon, Surrey CR2 7NL (01–657 5740).

If you choose a garment, don't be surprised if she rings up to check on your skirt length! 'So many folk trip up on this measurement,' she says, 'and please ask them to *print* their name and address.' Above: *deep, striped cuffs, longish top and striped skirt give a fluid line to this 'astrakhan' two-piece, knitted in purl stitch in 70% acrylic, 30% nylon. This one was made to measure for Amanda. At £59, it can be made in any combination of cream, flame or brown. By Anne Kent.*

(Reproduced by kind permission of *Family Circle* magazine)

B Sleeping Beauties

To allow sleeping dolls to lie in luxury, Pat Harrison and Sue Muttit dreamed up this delightful hand-made sleeping nest.

Pat and Sue were making babies' quilts when they discovered a demand for scaled-down bedding for dolls. Now their dolls' nests are proving real winners. The nests are usually made up in three basic sizes, though variations can be made by special request. The small size takes up to a 7in (18cm) doll — fits Carrie and Christopher dolls — and costs £1.95 inc p&p. The medium size (fits Tiny Tears-sized dolls) is £3, and the large size (for baby-sized dolls or even small-sized babies) is £4.80.

Instructions for making a medium-sized nest are given right, but if you'd like to order one ready-made, please write to Sue Muttit at 14 South Road, Hagley, West Midlands DY9 0JT.

Tips from Pat and Sue

Discovering the right outlet for crafts is all-important. We find playgroup coffee mornings and charity fairs are some of the best ways of selling our work. We agree in advance to give about 10% of takings to any charity concerned.

You must use good-quality materials. Elastic must be able to withstand fairly rough handling; fabric needs to be lightweight and soft enough to gather well; wadding should be washable.

To adapt the nest to different-sized dolls, cut the original strips of fabric twice the length of the doll. Adjust widths to fit.

Making a Medium-sized Nest

1   Cut two pieces of fabric and one piece of wadding all 12 x 32in (30 x 81cm). Pin together, right sides facing; polyester wadding beneath. Round off corners at one end.

2   Stitch round, leaving a small opening at side

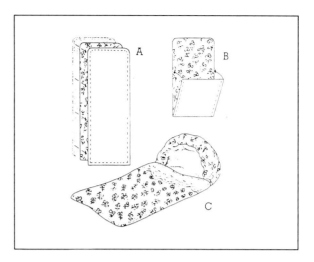

(Diagram A). Trim seams, turn through, enclosing wadding. Stitch opening to close.

3   Stitch trimming to short straight edge of patterned side.

4   Fold up ⅓ of bag. Stitch a 1in (2.5cm) seam down each side (Diagram B). Turn through.

5   Gather hood with double-thickness shirring elastic through lining only. Stitch hood corners to bag (see C).

(Reproduced by kind permission of *Home & Freezer Digest*)

C Silk Splash

A lady with an eye for colour is making sure that it will be a bright and sunny summer with her off-beat printed silk scarves and ties. Anna Tilson, to whom we owe this splash of colour, designs and prints from Studio 152, 27 Clerkenwell Close, London EC1R 0AT. The small silk scarves are about £18, the large raw silk shawls are about £37 and the zany tie for a bold man, £10. Liberty of London W1 also have a selection in their 'One-Off' department.

(Reproduced by kind permission of *Company* magazine)

This sample press release will give you some idea of how to write one of your own.

Coming up Roses — A new craft venture in the Cambridgeshire Fenland. Three years ago city secretary Rona Chatteris would not have believed that in 1985 she would be living in the depths of the countryside, totally wrapped up in roses. But that is the only way to describe her life today. Since her marriage to her horticulturist husband, Leonard,

Rona finds that it's roses, roses all the way. While Leonard grows them she sketches them. She then turns her sketches into satin appliqué, and creates a complete range of rose-splashed, appliquéd, luxury lingerie — negligees, wraps, slips, bed-jackets and nightdresses — that are now being snapped up by top shops throughout the country, as well as being sold in New York.

With practically no training in needlework or art, apart from two 'pretty pathetic' O-levels, Rona is amazed by her success and can only explain it by the fact that she herself loves what she makes. To start with she created them only for her own pleasure, then found that her friends kept begging her to produce more to order, for themselves and *their* friends. Eventually a local shop approached her with an offer that was just too good to turn down, and from then on there has been no looking back. Now two of her neighbours help her with the cutting out and sewing up while she concentrates on her drawing, and on designing new lines. Satin sheets and pillow slips are the next things due for Rona's rose treatment. All the marketing and management of the venture is master-minded by her twin brother, Roger, so that she can stay at home with her drawing board, silks and satins.

Rona has no regrets at leaving the bustle and excitement of city life for the quiet of the country where the nearest shop is three miles away and the next bus probably next week. 'Everything's coming up roses,' she says. 'My days are spent looking at them, smelling them, touching them, drawing them . . . and *wearing* them!' What more could any girl want?

For further information, contact: Mrs Rona Chatteris, Chatteris Nurseries, Fen Acre, Cambridgeshire. Tel: 111 222 1212

However, quite apart from leaflets and brochures, advertisements and articles, photographs and drawings, if you make a good product it will sell itself much more effectively by its appearance rather than description, and one of the things you need to do quite urgently when you set up as a professional is to get your actual work *seen*. This can be a very simple process. I was told again and again, 'I made my own clothes and my children's and people saw them and asked me to make theirs,' or 'My friends wore my sweaters and brought me orders from their friends,' or, 'I made soft toys for Christmas presents and was flooded with orders for *next*

Christmas!' That's the most straightforward and often the most effective form of self-advertisement. But this can be taken several steps further. It is often possible to rent showing space — glass cases in hotel foyers, for example, or in arts centres, leisure centres, libraries or tourist information offices; or windows of banks or building societies; or even windows of business premises which are temporarily unused because the lease is changing hands. Be brave in ferreting out possible display areas. If you see advertising cases or useful windows that are being used either by other craftspeople, or by charitable concerns, or just standing empty, find out who is responsible for them, whether they are prepared to let you use them, and whether you can afford to use them. Even if the rent is quite high the outlay may still pay dividends. In one town I visited I walked past a High Street insurance office with a very prominent window. Tucked in one corner, in a space about the size of a tea-tray, were three enchanting crocheted swans and a grey fur-fabric seal, with a small card which read: 'Churcham Cottage Crafts, Tel: Churcham 333.' When I contacted the craftswoman I discovered that she was totally inundated with orders as a result of this modest little presentation. Everyone had seen her swans and they had become the talk of the town.

Another way of showing what you make is by giving talks or demonstrations to organisations like the Women's Institute, and the Townswomen's Guild, school groups, youth groups, Eventide groups and the National Housewives' Register. Speakers are always in demand, especially those who have something to show and can give their talk strong visual appeal. The speaker's fee is minimal, and it is not likely that many sales will be made as a direct result of the talk, but the indirect results are often valuable. The local paper usually reports the event, your name begins to get talked about, your reputation spreads, and useful contacts are made.

Closely allied to this, and an ideal showcase for those who make clothes of any kind, are fashion shows, organised with the help of, and in aid of, a good cause or local or national charity. These are usually great fun, raise valuable funds, and — whether you are making wedding dresses, silk lingerie, hats, maternity wear, children's clothes, outsize garments, fancy dress, sun suits or ski suits — there is normally a willing stream of models anxious to show off your garments, and friendly volunteers prepared to work for the event provided that their funds benefit. Again, the financial value as far as you are concerned is not direct, but it does get you known and talked about.

Ribbon Designs

Cushions.   Bedspreads.   Craft Kits.

42 Lake View,
Edgware
Middx. HA8 7RU   Tel. 01-958 4966

Margaret Granger

Embroidery & Watercolour Paintings

Ashtead 75486

Wherever you go, wherever you show, you should always take your business cards with you and scatter them like confetti. Later, when people are discussing the event, they may very well decide that they would like to contact you, and if they have no name and number to fall back on you could lose a potentially valuable order.

It is possible, for those very determined, to get started and get known the other way round. That is, instead of making a product and then finding a way of persuading people to buy it, they find out what people want to buy and then provide it. I came across two clever craftswomen who were

doing just that. Ena had two children at a local school of dancing where the pupils were required to wear navy blue leotards and pale pink leg-warmers and sweaters of a very basic design. Local chain stores sold dancewear that was adequate, but most of it was very expensive, didn't stand up to the frequent washing it needed, and wore out so rapidly that it couldn't be handed down or sold through the parents' clothes exchange scheme. Ena had a knitting-machine and her sister had just bought a sewing-machine. She rapidly calculated that between them they could make the required garments for two-thirds of the chain-store prices, use better quality yarn and fabric that would both wash and wear well, yet *still* earn a fair return for their time without even having to advertise or tout for business. She got the ballet teacher's permission to send out a duplicated leaflet to parents the next time the children had to take notes home about a forthcoming concert, and within hours her telephone was ringing and she was in business.

Angela was pregnant and making her own very pretty maternity wear — huge, exciting, and highly fashionable shirts, and lovely, baggy cotton overalls in icecream colours. When she went to her pre-natal classes and clinics she realised that her clothes were causing a minor sensation, so she handed out a card, offering to make similar outfits for the other mums-to-be, and calling herself by the clever name of 'Mum's The Word'. The orders came rolling in, too many for her to handle once she was delivered of twins, but by that time she was sufficiently established to have acquired a partner and two out-workers to keep the ball rolling.

Both Ena and Angela recognised a need; knew that they could fill it; made direct contact with a ready-made market which was not being effectively catered for in their area, and consequently created for themselves a lucrative and continuous selling outlet.

Good publicity of some sort is vital to any effective business venture, but it can range from the direct sort of publicity that says, 'Look at what I'm wearing; if you like it I can make one for you', to the more complicated sort which involves paid advertisements, hand-outs, press releases, public appearances, talks and demonstrations. How you publicise your own project depends largely upon:

What you make
where you live
what selling method you employ, and
whether you are aiming to earn a full salary or pocket money

It does need to be carefully thought out and planned, always bearing in mind your potential productivity. It's as bad to be over-stretched as under-stretched, and either can lead to financial disaster.

Nevertheless, in the end, the product sells itself. If you make something good, and you expose it to the sort of people who will like it, or need it, and can afford to pay for it, then it will be bought. This is, in essence, the secret of the phenomenal success of party-plan selling and craft fairs. If someone goes to a knitwear party the chances are that he or she is inclined to buy some knitwear, if it is attractive and properly priced. If people go to a craft fair they are presumably in the right frame of mind to buy crafts, provided that they see things that they like. But it's those provisos that are the critical factor. Whether the money actually changes hands depends upon the excellence and originality of the product, and its price, and all the advertising in the world is not going to change that. Success depends upon making a good thing, making it well, and costing it properly.

7 Outlets

There is no doubt that the craft world is blossoming today. After a spell in the wilderness, well-made, well-designed, hand-crafted goods are now in great demand, and if you have the skill to create them, the ability to organise your time and to rationalise your costing, and the initiative to go out and find your market, there is no reason at all why you shouldn't be able to sell, and make a profit. The list below shows just some of the needlecrafts that are being practised at present.

Knitting — machine or hand
Sewing — machine or hand
Weaving
Lacemaking
Crochet
Macramé
Ribbon-weaving
Patchwork
Quilting
Smocking
Embroidery — machine or hand
Appliqué
Beading
Tatting

Some of the objects or articles that can be produced from either one or a combination of these crafts are displayed overleaf. They fall into five main sections, but it's interesting to note how often one skill complements another. For instance, ribbon-weave can be used as decorative detail either by a dressmaker or curtain-maker; hand-made lace decorates clothes and soft-furnishings; quilting is ubiquitous and turns up on clothes, bedspreads, decorative wall-hangings, even shoes and slippers. In these cases either one craftsperson has to develop several related skills, the ribbon-weaver becoming a dressmaker, the shoemaker learning to quilt, or two craftspeople have to get together to combine their talents, as in the case of a fashion designer teaming up with a smocker to work on the same garment.

1   Knitwear

plain, traditional or novelty sweaters
tabards, waistcoats and jerkins
suits
dresses
coats
hats, hoods, balaclavas, cowls
shawls, scarves, stoles
gloves, mittens, legwarmers, socks, slipper-
  socks
children's and babywear
ties

KNITTED GOODS
cushions
bedspreads
rugs
wall-hangings

The items listed above are merely an indication of the sort of things that can be made by the skilled knitter. The complete range is enormous and expanding, and depends largely upon the craftsperson's imagination, creativity and capacity to develop ideas and diversify. A good example of this is to be seen in the huge variety of sweaters now available, and the various crazes that sweep the population. A short while ago there was a cult of sheep sweaters. It began with ordinary white sheep knitted into the design. It was followed by a black sheep sweater, one black one among all the white. The ultimate sheep sweater had a knitted picture of a sheep knitting a people sweater. When summer drove the sheep sweaters into the back of the wardrobe an enterprising craftsman produced a sheep tee-shirt to take its place, cotton printed with a sheep pattern. So successful was the sheep motif that it was followed up by pink elephant sweaters, and duck sweaters marketed under the catch phrase of 'Quite Quackers'. As long as sweaters remain a fashion garment the market is wide open for the next craze, and just waiting for some lucky person to produce a bright idea.

As well as picture sweaters, striped rainbow sweaters in vivid colours, and contemporary patterned sweaters, there are buyers in plenty for Arans, Shetlands, Guernseys, Bretons, Icelandics, and Fair Isles, and for traditional patterns like these knitted up in untraditional yarns such as silk, cotton, mohair or cashmere. Embroidered sweaters are also popular, as are those that have sequins, pearls, or silver and gold threads knitted in among the stitches. And there's a new vogue for appliquéd woollens in which the segments of a picture or pattern are knitted separately and superimposed on the garment in the manner of a collage. That's just the start of the story. The sweaters can be teamed up with co-ordinates such as skirts, scarves and gloves of the same design.

Alternatively, knitters can offer a service knitting or adapting any pattern that the customer cares to provide. Some designer-knitters will create a pattern specifically for a customer, working out a personalised logo or motif, if required, as well as the basic shape and design, a valuable service for clubs, groups and societies. Others put together a 'knit-kit' which may include the yarn, pattern, chart, designer's label, buttons or zips, and a photograph of the finished garment — everything except the needles needed to create an original.

It is also possible to create knitting patterns for magazines or the big wool firms, but they must be outstandingly good to get as far as that. If you want to try, are confident that the pattern works, that the design is good and original, and have made up a finished garment perfect in every detail, and if you have been able to work out a set of neatly typed and easy-to-follow instructions, telephone and make an appointment with either the knitting editor of the magazine which seems most likely to appreciate your work, or the chief designer of a wool firm whose patterns you yourself admire. You have little to lose, and a lot to gain if you are successful.

Finally, knitted cushions, bedspreads and wall-hangings can sell well provided that they are attractive enough, unusual and well made. Smart craft centres, and up-market shops like Liberty and Harrods, might show an interest in them, or, like clothes, they can be sold as a pattern to a magazine so that other women can have the pleasure of making them up. Magazine editors have told me that whenever they publish patterns for knitted cushions there is an enormous response from their readers.

2 Dressmaking

alteration and mending
made-to-measure garments
pattern-cutting

SPECIAL-OCCASION CLOTHES
wedding dresses
ball gowns
fancy dress
theatrical costumes
christening robes

SPECIAL-NEED CLOTHES
maternity clothes
outsize garments
lingerie, trousseau and nightwear
beach and sun-wear
pinafores, smocks and overalls
school uniforms

SPECIALLY DECORATED CLOTHES
hand-embroidered
smocked
pieced
beaded
painted
batik

dress trimmings, collars: in crochet, lace, ribbon
     work, etc
cuffs, belts

The Dream Factory, Friday Street,
Painswick, Gloucestershire GL6 6QJ.
Tel : (0452) 812379

This is an umbrella term that covers a whole range of needle skills — from the business of doing alterations and repairs and making up patterns for friends and neighbours to running a small couture firm. There are many ways of specialising within the dressmaking world. It's possible either to choose one type of clothing for which you have assured yourself there is a demand that you would like to supply, such as maternity wear, fancy dress or dolls' clothes; or to choose one particular type of fabric with which to work, such as fine leather or silk; or to concentrate on a particular type of decorative work incorporated into clothes, smocking, perhaps, or hand-embroidery, appliqué, quilting or patchwork. If you are very good at design and trained in pattern-cutting you may be able to sell your patterns by advertising them, along with illustrations, in fabric shops and sewing-machine suppliers' show-rooms. The proprietors are usually happy to co-operate — though they may charge you a commission fee.

It's important to have confidence in your design and sewing talents. If you have, you can go far, from quite modest beginnings. Willie Walters, Judy Dewsbury and Esme Young together make up a team known as 'Swanky Modes', and sell their own designs of zany, sexy clothes — disco dresses, evening wear, swimwear and daywear — from a cheerful but slightly scruffy shop in London's Camden Town. They've worked for years with scanty financial rewards and blatant criticism of some of their more outrageous designs. They've resolutely ignored complaints from feminists that 'these clothes degrade women' and from established fashion buyers who termed them 'punk'. They've learned, the hard way, to be business-like. 'When we started out,' says Willie, 'our approach to design was professional but our attitude to business was slap-happy. We've learned a lot during the hard times of the seventies.' Now, in their early thirties, they are beginning to grab the attention and admiration of the international fashion world and sell to top shops in Britain, the United States and Italy. In 1983 they won a *Woman* Fashion Award. They look as if they might strike it rich and if they do it will not be thanks to a vast back-up team of professional workers but to the husbands who share the domestic chores and childcare, and to their partners who take turns ferrying the children to and from school. They describe themselves simply as 'women working and coping'.

3 Accessory-making

gloves
hats
scarves
belts
shoes, slippers, boots, sandals
bags, purses, luggage
ties

Closely allied to dressmaking, and often going hand-in-hand, is accessory-making, and there continues to be a great demand for hand-crafted hats, scarves and bags, and even, surprisingly, shoes and boots. One enterprising venture is 'Marged Shoes', a women's co-operative that makes shoes, boots and sandals, in leather, canvas, or padded cotton. There are seven members, and they set up a shoemaking co-operative in Wales, in 1981, with no capital but with the support of many women who either loaned or gave them enough money to buy premises, machinery and materials. Their aims are to earn themselves a modest living; to make strong, reasonably priced shoes for women; and, if possible, to provide more jobs for women in the locality. They are a group of inventive, skilled and determined women, as their name implies. The original Marged was born in 1696 and lived to be 105. She was a first-rate carpenter, blacksmith, tailor, lamp-maker, fiddle-maker, musician *and* shoemaker, and at the age of 70 she could still out-wrestle every man in Wales. That's the sort of versatility and courage they reckon they need to succeed.

48

4 Soft Furnishings, Home Accessories, Personal Gifts

furniture upholstery and loose covers

curtains and window-blinds
bedspreads and quilts
bedlinen
bedroom accessories: laundry bags, nightdress cases, hot-water-bottle covers, tissue-box covers
dining-room and kitchen goods: table linens and place-mats, napkins, tea-, coffee-, egg-cosies, covers for coffee machine, food mixer, toaster, bread-roll holders, pan holders and oven-gloves, peg-bags
living-room accessories: foot-stools, draught-excluders, bean-bags, cushions and floor-cushions, screens and fire-screens, lamp-shades, rugs and wall-hangings, murals, collages, embroidered pictures and fabric photograph frames

personal gift items: padded clothes-hangers, lavender and herb bags and pillows, silk flowers and ribbon bouquets, silk ties, peg dolls, book-marks and spectacle cases, shoe-bags, knitting bags, work bags and baskets, pincushions and needlecases

There always seems to be a market for craft work to enhance the home, whether it's a matter of making up curtains and loose covers for neighbours, or creating heirloom quilts and embroidered or appliquéd pictures to sell in the super-stores of Knightsbridge. These dovetail neatly with the smaller soft-ware that make such good gifts — napkins, oven-gloves, lavender bags, pyjama cases. Cushions, in particular, are sure sellers because they are both useful and decorative, and one can never have too many. During my interviews I found them made in all shapes and sizes, in a multitude of techniques — knitted, painted, appliquéd, embroidered, lace-trimmed, quilted, woven from ribbons, made from patchwork or batik, shaped into novelty designs like animals, or even icecream cones, scented with herbs and pot-pourri. There was no end to the variety, whether they were tiny scatter cushions to pile on the bed or sofa, or huge floor cushions and bean-bags to double as extra seating.

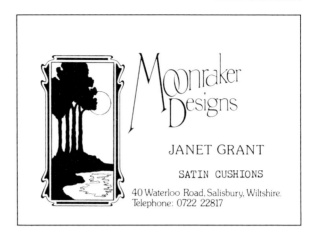

Moonraker Designs

JANET GRANT

SATIN CUSHIONS

40 Waterloo Road, Salisbury, Wiltshire.
Telephone: 0722 22817

In this area one can be as original and inventive as one dares. The most extraordinary idea I came across was that produced by 'Woolly Bloomers', a bright young husband-and-wife team who make *knitted* pot plants, daffodils, narcissi, tulips, and — the biggest seller of all — lovely hairy cacti. One of their friends handled their publicity with great skill, and a clever press release combined with the sheer silliness of the notion caught the attention of the media and got them wide coverage and booming, blooming, sales. Because of their careful timing a Woolly Bloomer pot plant became the cult Christmas gift of 1983 and has gone on to bigger and better business ever since.

Similarly, silk flowers are very much in vogue, and you can charge high prices for them because they are such a luxury. There are classes available in flower-making at adult education centres, but this craft can be self-taught with the help of books (see Appendix 1) and soon you'll find that once you have the knack they are quick and easy to make. They can be sold through craft shops, gift shops and department stores, and also to florists who quite enjoy using them to complement their fresh blooms. Silk ribbon bridal bouquets are becoming more and more popular with brides who want a permanent memento of their big day, and this craft is ideally suited to the home-based craft worker. If you make them it might be worth your while advertising your service in one of the magazines such as *Brides* or *Wedding Day* which are aimed purely at brides-to-be and their families, or better still, try to persuade one of their feature writers to give you a mention along with a good illustration of your work. Alternatively, you could take a stand at a wedding festival if you can find one in your area — if your display is pretty enough you are bound to attract custom. Or it may be that you could persuade a wedding dress shop in the locality to show some of your bouquets and posies to enhance their gowns, and to take personal orders for you on a mutually agreed commercial basis. They have, after all, got nothing to lose and everything to gain because you are helping them to set off their own stock to advantage without it costing them a penny.

5   Soft-toymaking

soft toys
glove, arm and finger puppets
fabric mobiles
dolls and dolls' clothes
treasure cots

Finally, the other demand which never ceases is for good, original, well-made soft toys. The major problem in this field is safety, and the British Standards Institution lays down standards which cover matters such as inflammability, security of eyes, safe filling materials, protection of sharp edges, and so on. You should check the requirements in an HMSO leaflet called 'Toy Safety Regulations, S.I. 1974 Number 1367' available either from the library or from:

HMSO
PO Box 569
London SE1 9NH

and also go along to a reference library and look at a book called Code of Safety Requirements for Children's Toys and Playthings which is a British Standards document, number 3443. Alternatively, the Citizens' Advice Bureau might be able to give you all the information you need.

It would also be wise to contact:

British Toymakers' Guild
4 Ruvigny Gardens
London SW15 1JR
(Tel: 01–788 4273)

since its aim is to foster the craft of making good soft toys that are safe.

It may be tempting to ignore this red tape, but beware. If a customer complains you could be prosecuted either by the Trading Standards Office or the Environmental Health Department. If you are creating a serious business from toymaking it might be worth sending a sample to the British Standards Institute for testing. Enquire first about the procedure and fee from:

British Standards Institute
Linford Wood
Milton Keynes MK14 6LE
(Tel: 0908 320066)

It's also a wise precaution to take out extra insurance to cover yourself in the case of accident since you, as the manufacturer, are responsible for any illness or injury caused by faulty toys. I know from personal experience that this really is a problem which frequently occurs. When I ran my own craft shop I had soft toys from a very reputable, long-established, cottage-industry firm removed from my shelves because a Trading Standards official claimed that the eyes weren't firmly secured, and a complaint from an irate customer whose baby had bitten off and devoured a rabbit's fluffy tail within five minutes of receiving the gift.

The one aspect of a hand-crafted soft toy that makes it a seller despite the competition from cheap, mass-produced toys is its individuality. Whether you are adapting paper patterns, or creating your own design, there should be some difference, some mark of originality. It is important anyway to avoid slavishly copying anything else on the market as this could cause problems with the copyright of patterns. You must also beware of making toys that represent characters from books or television or films because officially they can only be manufactured under licence. Think of something novel, and you are

Plate 3 A traditional English agricultural round smock from Bridget Lapsley, Flocks & Smocks; patchwork cushion covers from Anna Potten (the covers showing houses were worked as commissions); painted and hand-embroidered sheep picture from Margaret Granger

halfway there. One enterprising craftswoman I came across made scented dolls, clowns and mobiles. The combination of fragrance, movement, and the shining colours of the fabrics she used, made the market stall from which she sold her wares totally irresistible, glowing and vibrating with twisting silver moons and stars, golden suns, and gorgeous satin rainbows.

If you come up with an idea that is new and attractive but basically simple, you might even get it accepted by a magazine or pattern company, provided that you can compile concise, easy-to-follow instructions. There are many books available to start you thinking and trigger off your ideas, as well as advising you about methods and techniques, and

The British Toy and Hobby Manufacturers'
    Association
80 Camberwell Road
London SE5 0EG

publishes a directory which gives the names and addresses of suppliers of eyes, noses and other accessories. Some are also listed in Appendix 6.

Ways of Selling

Once you have decided what you want to make, are sure that you can make it well, and have ascertained that there is a demand for your product, the next step is to consider how and where to sell it. There is a whole range of possibilities, some of which have been referred to in the previous pages.

Personal Selling
The first, and simplest method is to sell to friends, neighbours and local people through word of mouth and perhaps a little bit of advertising in a local paper or shop window. You must be your own sales person by wearing or using

Plate 4   Hand-painted roller blind, and appliquéd cot quilt, from Selma Harris; children's clothes from Sue Manners, Suzy Q; matinée jacket from Ann Kinsey; baby changing bag from Judy More; hippo from Rusty Grimmond, Rustoys

what you make and letting it be seen that it is excellent. Wear your own hand-made clothes or dress your children in them, so that people admire and want something similar for themselves. If you make curtains or cushions, make sure that the curtains and cushions in your own home are superb and enviable. If you make toys, cot quilts, baby-bags or layettes, give some occasionally as presents — they're bound to be admired and shown off to friends. Always let it be known that you are in the market for orders and commissions. Have confidence in your skill, be proud of it, and you will be your own public relations officer. It always pays dividends.

There may well be specialist shops in your area that can be of help. For instance, a dry-cleaning firm would probably put up your advertisement saying that you are available to do alterations and replace zips. A fabric shop would advertise the fact that you are prepared to make up curtains, or clothes from people's own patterns and material, a wool shop may spread the word that you are a skilled knitter. A local school notice-board might well give you space to tell parents that you can make items of made-to-measure school uniform, a boon to busy or unskilled mothers who can't make their children's clothes for them.

Mail Order
When you feel established and confident you may like to broaden your horizons and advertise in the sort of magazine or newspaper that is most appropriate to your craft, and cast your net further afield. See Appendix 2 for magazines to consider. From there the next step is into the mail order business, probably with an advertisement and a press release, but before you go as far as that you should make quite sure that you are able to deal with a large number of orders should there be a large demand. Nothing is more irritating than ordering something special, perhaps for a gift for an important occasion, and then finding that the delivery time is too lengthy to meet the deadline. And from the craftsman's point of view it can be enormously frustrating to have the possibility of a large number of sales but no chance of satisfying the enquiries. To avoid this it may be necessary to have the

Unique Carpet Bags made in our studios in Suffolk, England, with the care, craftsmanship and quality that are rare these days. Each bag is different, created from an almost infinite variety of pattern, colour and texture inherent in carpets. With our special treatment of double washing with pure soap, the selected pieces of old carpet maintain their strength whilst becoming beautifully soft.

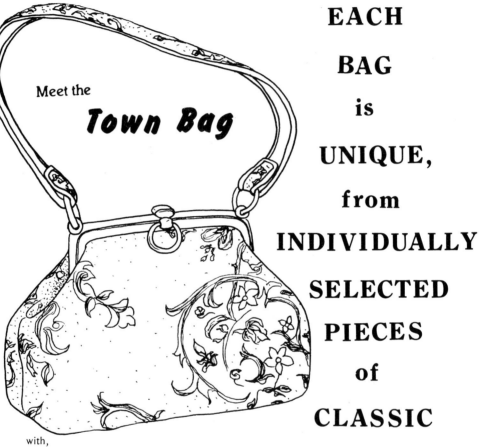

Meet the
Town Bag

EACH BAG is UNIQUE, from INDIVIDUALLY SELECTED PIECES of CLASSIC CARPETS

with,

★ Carpet Strap

★ Strong Frame In Bright Nickel Or Antiqued Finish

★ Copious Loose Lining In Cotton Or Poly/Cotton

★ Double Stitched Seams, Triple Stitched Corners, Using Tough Thread

★ Approx: 16 x 10 inches

and, of course,

We willingly exchange any bag that does not meet your marketing aesthetic

Loretta Quartey   Harrick Hart

54

services of one or two outworkers to help you. Mail order can become very big business. Richard and Julia Searight work with a group of a hundred knitters to produce home-made sweaters to sell through their catalogue. They also hand-knit the customers' own patterns, as well as offering co-ordinating skirts, scarves and gloves. Needless to say, a project the size of this one requires a great deal of organisation and back-up, but it is possible to start on a much smaller scale and make a success of it.

Craft Fairs
Many craftsmen find that craft fairs are a comparatively easy and lucrative way of selling their wares. The only overheads are the cost of the stall and the transport of their goods, plus the expense of dressing the stall to make it look as attractive as possible, and they can be assured of a steady flow of customers ready and willing to buy provided that the goods are not too highly priced. If you are into the expensive luxury trade this may not be the best place for you, because what you are looking for at a fair is the impulse buyer, in holiday mood, with money in his or her pocket. You will find a calendar of craft fairs and similar events, such as agricultural shows, steam rallies, summer festivals, in *Crafts* magazine, and many are advertised in the section 'Craft Fairs and Forthcoming Events' in the back pages of *Popular Crafts.* Some, of course, are much better than others. The only way to make sure that a particular event is right for you is to go along the first time as an observer, or to talk to other craftspeople who have had a stall on previous occasions.

Craft Exhibitions
Craft exhibitions are closely allied to craft fairs, but they tend to be rather more exclusive and will accept only work of very high quality of both workmanship and design. Often they are put on in arts or crafts centres, or under the auspices of the Crafts Council, the regional arts associations, the Rural Crafts Association, the county Guilds of Craftsmen, or the specific crafts guilds. If you are a member of a group such as the Quilters' Guild, or the Embroiderers' Guild, or if you belong to something like the Rural Crafts

Association or the Guild of Gloucestershire Craftsmen, the secretary will keep you informed of their exhibitions and your eligibility to show your work in them. This is not an automatic member's privilege in many cases — there may be selection procedures to go through. If you don't belong to an organisation you will have to do some research yourself, writing off to your own regional arts association, asking at your local arts or crafts centre, following up some of the leads given in *Crafts* magazine, until you find and make your own opportunity. The advantage of exhibiting is not just to make immediate sales, or even to benefit from the prestige it bestows. The real value lies in getting your work seen, appreciated, talked about, noticed and known. Many of the craftspeople I interviewed had been given valuable media coverage in local and national papers, or had been sought out by the buyers of galleries and shops, through having had their work on show in an exhibition.

Sometimes exhibitions are put on by our great stately homes, or by the National Trust, or by groups of craftsmen simply getting together and hiring a beautiful place from which to show and sell their things, and they are nearly always an impetus to work and create in a disciplined way, working to a time-table, and often trying out new ideas and techniques, while at the same time achieving an extremely high level of craftsmanship. Get to know what happens in your area — the local library and newspaper will both be helpful sources of information — and find out how you can get involved. You might even find one or two other craftspeople with complementary skills who will join forces so that you can put on your own exhibition in a local library, theatre foyer, or restaurant. It only needs initiative and effort to get the ball rolling. Usually the initial expense of hiring your space, publicising the event, and providing wine for a private view, is rapidly recouped in sales and private commissions, provided that you show your work to maximum advantage and invite the right people to come along and see it, people who will appreciate what you have to offer and will be able to afford to buy it. Before you take this step it is sensible to go to other exhibitions, get yourself invited to some private views, and watch very carefully exactly how it is organised and managed, so that you can make a success of it when your turn comes. And always remember to keep your standards as high as possible, because an exhibition is a shop window for excellence.

Market Stalls

Alternatively, you might like to take a stall in a regular commercial market, either a general market or one which specialises in crafts. These are places which usually do booming business. In London, the famous Jubilee Market in Covent Garden, the Camden Lock market, and the smaller street markets, attract thousands of sightseers and customers every weekend, and there are hundreds of others spread throughout the country. Scrutinise your locality and your local paper to see which would be the best place for you, then go along and have a chat to the market supervisor to find out when a stall would be available and what it would cost. Make a few enquiries and observations about conditions, too — the other stall-holders will be a fund of useful information. Remember that covered markets are one thing, open ones quite another. It is no joke, and it can be a disaster, to have your beautiful wares exposed to wind and weather. When you eventually have your own stall make sure that it is as attractive and eye-catching as possible, and that you have cards, price-lists and brochures, preferably illustrated, for people to take home and mull over. Many don't want to make an instant purchase, but will come back later if they like what they've seen, especially when Christmas begins to loom up.

Women's Institute Market

The other sort of market-selling is through the excellent Women's Institute markets. You don't need to be a member of the WI, or even a woman, to sell through their organisation, merely a shareholder in the local Market Society, and this will cost you 5p for life membership! Two booklets, 'The WI Market Handbook', and 'Markets, Pleasure and Profit', will give you all the information you need. Both are available from The National Federation of Women's Institutes, 39 Eccleston Street, London SW1 9NT. Standards of workmanship must be very high and

have to be scrutinised by a controller before they are accepted. The controller or one of her craft specialists will advise you on labelling and presenting your work, and fixing a price, part of which will be deducted as commission for the WI. This is not a way to make a lot of money because profits are relatively small. It is, however, a way to learn a lot about making and selling, and also to be part of a movement which gives an enormous amount of moral support, friendship and camaraderie to those who are involved in it. It must be admitted, though, that some WI markets are better than others, friendlier and more efficiently organised. It is sensible to find out several in your area and to visit them all to see what sort of atmosphere they create, how busy and prosperous they are, and what sort of things they sell, before you approach the controller of the one of your choice and show her your craft.

Party-plan Selling

This is another successful selling method that takes a lot of organising but does not involve you in expensive overheads. The method is to persuade a friend to put on a selling party for you in her house and to invite as many people as possible to come along and buy, either at the party or by special order. The party hostess receives a commission on your sales, and the whole project snowballs as people who have been to a party and enjoyed it volunteer to have another in *their* home. Party selling is an American idea that has worked with household equipment, jewellery, leather goods, even sex aids, and is now being used to great effect for underwear, children's clothes, knitwear, and so on. Sometimes a craftsperson can team up with a charity organisation which will hold the party in return for a percentage of the profits and the useful publicity it gives them. Sometimes groups of craftsmen get together and sell together so that the organisation does not fall on one pair of shoulders and the variety of goods attracts more people. Very often selling and advertising is much easier if craftspeople band together and share their skills and facilities instead of relying entirely on their own resources, and it's good for the morale, too.

Selling parties tend to succeed provided that:

sufficient interested people turn up, who are there to buy rather than just join in the fun
the goods have been carefully selected and costed to appeal to the buyers' taste, needs, and pocket
the items for sale are attractively displayed
the party is well-enough organised to be a thoroughly enjoyable event

I went to a knitwear party which was a feast to the eyes. Beautiful sweaters hung from hi-tech scaffolding, or were displayed stylishly on wooden stretchers. Coloured photographs of the knitwear being worn by the knitters themselves decorated the walls. Huge swathes of brilliantly coloured wool spilled out of wicker baskets, dazzling the eye. Wine flowed, soft music played, flowers filled the rooms, and the three women who made the sweaters wandered among their guests with their pattern books, price-lists, order forms and tape measures, laughing and chatting among friends while they modelled their own lovely clothes. In such an atmosphere it was almost impossible *not* to buy.

The children's-clothes party I was invited to was entirely different. Toddlers scrambled around the floor playing with a pile of toys, or obediently stood still for half a minute to be measured, while their mothers talked to the dressmaker, flicked through the garments on her dress-rail, and examined her pattern cards. It was all very relaxed and informal. Tea flowed instead of wine, children's laughter took the place of soft music, and the noise was colossal, but it was right for the occasion and a lot of business was transacted, in a friendly, chatty fashion.

Retail Shops
You may prefer to sell direct to shops, galleries and crafts centres. If so, make sure that the shops you approach are the right sort of shops, where your work would be appreciated by customers and properly displayed and promoted by the sales team. Crafts are big business today and many retail outlets are on the look-out for well-designed, properly made goods, especially if they are a little different from the run-of-the-mill. There's nothing to be lost in going into a shop you admire, showing the owner or buyer your work, naming a realistic price and seeing what reaction you get. Some will only take your goods on a sale-or-return basis. If you agree to this try to establish that it should only be for a trial period and that if the first order sells well you would like the second order to be paid for on a more business-like basis. And try to satisfy yourself that the shops you sell to are on a sound financial footing and you will actually get your money. Bad debts can put the small business out of business. Prompt payment is vital to your cash flow, since if you don't get the money for one lot of goods you might find it difficult to buy materials to make the next lot of goods. Don't necessarily think that because you are a free-lance and not part of a large organisation you should sell only to small shops. I was amazed to discover how many craftspeople are sufficiently self-confident to go straight to the 'top shops', and how often names such as Liberty, Harrods and Peter Jones were offered to me as their *first* port of call. I was even more amazed to discover how often it paid dividends. 'I took one to show the buyer at Harrods and she took a dozen straight away,' I was told, again and again. It's true that shops of this calibre are always interested in anything that is first rate as far as materials, workmanship and design are concerned, so it pays to go 'up-market' if yourself are convinced that what you are making is excellent. But if you are not convinced you won't be able to convince anyone else. Self-assurance is the essence of successful selling.

Renting Selling Space
Another alternative is to hire your own selling space for a short time. It is possible, for example, to hire a room in the village hall from which to display and sell your wares. This can work very well if:

your initial advertising and publicity is excellent, and you have inundated the locality and your friends and neighbours with leaflets, posters and advertisements as well as persuading the local paper to write a little feature about your venture
the hall is centrally situated near the shopping centre
you put up eye-catching posters and boards out-

side to attract passing trade as well as those who have been notified in advance

you display your goods with as much panache as possible

you choose the right time to go public

A cold February Monday is unlikely to tempt any but your most loyal friends out of doors, but on a warm weekend in summer, or in the frantic run-up to Christmas, lots of customers will be glad to drop in and will be more in a mood to buy, with the usual proviso that you are making crafts which have popular appeal and affordable prices.

Many craftspeople find that this is the ideal way to sell. They spend several months working to get together enough stock to make a good display, sell it quickly and easily with minimal overheads provided that the rental for the hall isn't exorbitant, then have enough capital and several more months to prepare for their next sales day. In the meantime they will probably have picked up quite a few special orders and personal commissions to bring them in a little income over the intervening period. Village and community halls are not the only venues that can be used. Some enterprising individuals hire well-situated shops that are up for sale and standing empty, and open up for a Friday and Saturday to cash in on weekend shoppers.

Van Sales
If you can find the capital to invest in a van, and are able to drive it or find a driver-partner, you might like the idea of running a mobile shop. This selling method is great fun but it's better suited to a partnership of at least two, if not three, if it's going to work effectively without exhausting you, because the effort of organisation, selling and driving can be overwhelming for an individual. It is an excellent idea for remote rural areas, or huge housing estates, where shopping facilities and transport are minimal and many people are able to make only rare visits to their nearest large shopping centre. It brings an interesting event into the lives of the inhabitants and is bound to arouse the interest of the local media and so provide free publicity.

There is absolutely no point, of course, in simply driving into a village, parking your vehicle, opening the doors and saying 'come and buy'. The customers just won't be there. This sort of venture needs a carefully orchestrated advertising campaign, with posters in the village shop and elsewhere before you arrive, and if possible, door-to-door leafleting as well, telling the public exactly what you are selling, and where, and when. You should also check with the local police to make sure that you are not breaking any by-laws. But it *can* work. Two housewives from Dartington take their home-made children's clothes round the Devon villages in a van and sell them successfully. In a way it can be a variation on the party-plan method, with you showing patterns and taking orders for made-to-measure clothes in selected materials. The only difference is that you take the party with you instead of holding it in a friend's house. But it needs immaculate preparation and efficiency. Leave your tape-measure or pattern book at home and you could find yourself in trouble. Note that this method of selling is *only* suitable for places devoid of shops which might sell your type of goods. If you park your van full of knitwear outside a shop that sells sweaters you will bring down the wrath not only of rate-paying local shop-keepers but also of the local authority. If in doubt, get in touch with the authority and use your sales technique to sell the idea to them as an added amenity for their area rather than a get-rich-quick technique to line your own pocket. The Citizens' Advice Bureau will help you with information and addresses.

Renting Work Space
Another selling method to consider is to operate your business from rented premises. The best way of doing this, if possible, is to take studio/workshop space in an established arts or crafts centre, or in a centre for small businesses where craftspeople and small manufacturers can band together, sharing premises and costs. Opportunities of this sort are becoming widely available, partly due to individual and government efforts to help people to make a living from their own efforts and initiative in a period of high unemployment. Jane Playford, the lacemaker, explains in her interview in Chapter 10 the ad-

vantages of being situated in a centre like Wroxham Barns in Norfolk, which was converted from dereliction to make work and selling space for craftsmen. Anna Potten founded her textile business from Salisbury Arts Centre and found it possible to sell continuously through the arts centre circuit. In London there is a successful venture called Barley Mow Workspace which houses 150 small businesses, each with its own self-contained unit, including 'Woolgatherers' run by Liz Jones who makes and sells a beautifully designed collection of sweaters. Costs can be as low as £1,800 a year for a full business back-up, and people who could not otherwise have managed to set up on their own have been able to pool their resources and organise themselves into success through co-operation. A similar scheme is Metropolitan Workshops at Hackney, an initiative launched to create jobs and revitalise derelict areas at the same time. In this instance 250 craftsmen are housed in a converted hospital, and their rents can be as little as £10 a week. One of them is fashion designer, Jeanette Elahar, who shares studio space with other textile designers. The Duncan Craft Workshops, founded in 1980 in Otley, Yorkshire, are based on a similar idea of communal support, and house textile workers among their potters, jewellers and glass-blowers. At present they are converting buildings on their 200-year-old mill site for more craftsmen, and have shops and other amenities to attract visitors and tourists to buy their wares. Similar projects frequently search out craftspeople through advertisements like this from *Crafts* magazine: 'Workshops available in rural crafts centre. Edge New Forest, from £6 a week, friendly co-operative atmosphere.' From the depths of the leafy countryside to the heart of the industrial centres, if you live in a redundant steel area you will find that British Steel provides a number of 'managed workshop schemes'. You could even start up a similar project of your own, teaming up with other crafts people to share a large, interesting building, and to run services and sales to your common benefit. If you want to know more about this, contact Goddard Associates who are the acknowledged experts. Their telephone number is 01–994 6477.

Opening Your Own Shop

Going-it-alone from your own business premises can be daunting but not impossible, especially if you can turn part of your house into a shop, though you must observe planning procedures, safety requirements, insurance, and so on, as outlined in Chapter 3. If you want to rent or buy special business premises it is a much more ambitious and costly project. Basically, since your interest is presumably in craft rather than business, a shop should either be the centre for the sale of goods made by you and your outworkers, and be staffed by several people whether they are partners, or employees, or a group working together, so that you can find time to continue with your craftmanship; or a combined workshop and selling space where you can practise and demonstrate your skills and build up your stock as well as making money out of them. Some local authorities, as well as CoSIRA, can be helpful in letting premises to new firms, or there may be help at hand if you live in an enterprise zone. At present there are zones at Invergordon, Clydebank, Tyneside, Hartlepool, Salford, Wakefield, Belfast, Speke, Dudley, Corby, Swansea, and the Isle of Dogs in East London. Support comes in the form of simplified rates and planning controls as well as 100 per cent tax relief on the cost of new buildings. To find out if you are in a zone, and whether you could get help, contact your local authority. The alternative is to keep your eyes open, and scan the advertisements in papers and estate agents for shops in your area either for sale or to rent. Overheads can be enormous, though, and at present small shops are closing by the dozen every day, so don't invest your savings in a project of this sort unless you have done your research and costings with enormous care and are convinced that your sales will be sufficiently high to pay for your outgoings *and* bring you in an income worth all the hassles.

Combined Selling Methods

In practice, most craftspeople rely not on one, but on several methods of selling their goods. They might have their own shop, and sell on commission and through exhibitions. They might sell through party plan and markets. They might combine selling to retail outlets and through mail order. The permutations are endless and depend largely on what the craftsman makes, where he or she lives, and what sort of sales methods most appeal to them. Maggie Young is a knitwear manufacturer who has opened a shop called 'Over the Rainbow' on the Isle of Skye. She employs two dozen outworkers and sells both through her shop and through a mail-order catalogue, and she's combining the two so successfully that her turnover is reaching £60,000 a year. Dorothy Greenwood, whose commercial name is 'Knit-In', sells her made-up designer sweaters to Harrods and to retail outlets in France and the United States as well as accepting private commissions. Recently she diversified and launched her first mail-order 'knit-kit', a children's jumper called 'Canal Scene', because she felt that there was room on the market for a well-designed children's sweater kit. This was so successful an undertaking that she went on to create five more kits to follow the first prototype within a few months. Harrick Hart of Carpet Bags sells to retail shops, and through country fairs and festivals, but he also has an agent, selling the bags for him on a commission basis. And he's always working on new ideas.

Variety is not only the secret of the craftsman's satisfaction with his or her chosen way of life, and often the main factor in persuading them to opt for the insecurity of working as a freelance creator rather than joining in the safer nine-till-five routine of more conventional employment. It can also be the secret of commercial success if applied to marketing techniques. But there is no escaping the fact that it involves an enormous amount of discipline, determination, imagination, courage, and, most of all, a great deal of hard work.

8 Marketing and Organisation

The financial success of your crafts business — whether you are aiming to make it a pocket money venture or a full income earner — depends to a large extent upon the way in which you buy your basic materials; use your time; control your overhead expenditure; and build up good, business-like arrangements with your customers.

Marketing

It makes sense to buy your materials in bulk at wholesale prices, even if this may involve you in arranging with your bank manager to have an overdraft facility to get you going. There are many very reliable wholesale suppliers. Some are listed in Appendix 6. Others advertise in magazines such as *Drapers Record, Popular Crafts,* and *Pins and Needles.* Some have attractive discounts, seasonal sales and special offers that are worth cashing in on. Obviously, if you are ordering by post the first time it is wise to reply only to advertisements which carry the rider 'Money Back If Not Satisfied', but once you have found suppliers who suit your needs and

give good service at competitive prices it is worth sticking with them.

Another way of finding suppliers is to go to the big trade fairs such as: The British Craft Trade Fair, at Harrogate; The International Craft and Hobby Fair, at Wembley; The British Toy and Hobby Fair, at Earls Court; and Needlecraft, put on by the British Needlecrafts Council, all of which are widely advertised in the appropriate crafts magazines; or to buy *Popular Crafts' Guide to Good Craft Suppliers* (see Appendix 1). It is possible to buy bargain materials at markets, and at Brick Lane in the East End of London where the marker dealers buy their fabrics. Once it was the home of the Jews and the Huguenot weavers; now it has become a Bangladeshi ghetto with its associated rag trade, very busy and colourful. There are two problems of street buying. Firstly, there is no come-back if the fabric is faulty, and unless you make stringent checks *before* you part with your money you could have wasted it. If a customer complains and wants reimbursing, it is you who will carry the can and no one else. Secondly, if the material is good, and popular, you cannot guarantee getting the same thing again, so customers who want an exact replica are likely to be disappointed. Nevertheless, there are amazing bargains to be had for those with an eye to pick them out, so it is worth examining the market treasure trove.

The other bargain hunter's paradises are the end-of-season sales held in the big department stores when they are clearing out their winter tweeds and woollens to make room for their summer cottons, and vice versa. To take advantage of these you must be able to wait several months to see a return on the money you have laid out; have room to store fabrics or made-up goods until the next season comes round; and have the fashion or design sense not to buy material that will look dated by the time you want to sell it.

Plain-coloured or classically designed fabrics rarely date. The problems arise when buying patterned materials, since one year it may be the rage to be romantic, with flowers and pastel prints blooming on clothes, cloths and curtains, while the next year the demand may be for geometrical designs and brash, bold colour mixes.

It is common practice among the craftsmen I interviewed to have a 'bank' of material which has been bought not because it was needed but because it was beautiful and well priced, then stacked away until a use is found for it. Very often it's the love of fabrics that comes first and dominates the nature of the actual product. Janet Grant of Moonraker Designs collected her satin oddments before she worked out what to do with them. Ann Kinsey is a knitter because she loves wool. Jo Palmer's luxury Dream Factory clothes are dominated by her passion for sumptuous silks, velvets and laces (see Chapter 10). The magpie urge to snap up a bargain, or to buy something lovely just to put away until the time is ripe, serves many a craftsperson well in the initial stages of making money from his/her skill. Often it is possible to make the first batch of goods largely from fabric 'put by', and then use the money made from that first sale to plough back into materials for the next.

Making

It is obviously good business sense to create a range of goods designed to use up *all* the materials you buy instead of wasting lots of little left-overs. So, a knitter can make matching mittens or hats from the wool left over from sweaters; a toymaker may use the fur fabric scraps from a 3ft teddy bear to make a tiny, pocket-sized, baby bear; remnants of dress material can be transformed into matching, padded, scented clothes-hangers, or dolls' clothes, or a whole variety of bags — peg-bags, lavender bags, dorothy bags, shoe-bags, all of which are good selling lines.

The first lesson of marketing is to buy carefully, at competitive prices, and to use up all that you buy. This last point is more important than many people realise, and not only because of the economy aspect. It is always sensible to have a 'bread-and-butter' line as well as a prestige line — a product that will sell quickly and easily and give a rapid return on financial outlay, as well as one that is satisfying and challenging to make. By all means make hand-framed woollen suits that you can sell at £150 each, but these are a luxury item and sales may be steady but not brisk, to start with anyway. If you want a healthy, constant cash flow it will be worth making gloves and leg-warmers as well. Elizabeth Mann, from Essex, makes and dresses exquisite, expensive, period dolls to sell from her weekend market stall — but she also sells cheap and cheerful Miss Muffet spiders to keep the customers interested and the money flowing in. 'Quick cash,' she calls them. Jenny Lister, from Banbury, makes glorious embroidered bedspreads. They take months to finish, and she sells only one a year, but she has a regular outlet in two local shops for her pretty handkerchiefs that sell at £1 each and in such large numbers that she cannot keep up with the demand.

But it is a mistake to get so carried away by the cheap lines that sell easily and quickly that the quality crafts are neglected. For instance, you can work yourself to a standstill selling dozens of novelty felt book-marks at 20p each while the profit from the sale of only one felt-covered foot-stool or pouffe priced at £20 can be greater and the comparative artistic satisfaction immense. On the other hand, it may be the eager crowd snapping up bargain book-marks which attracts the customer with £20 to spend in the first place. Enthusiastic buyers invariably attract more — an empty shop or a neglected stall is always inhibiting.

Another important consideration is that big, luxury items which *look* expensive and can therefore command high prices are often less costly to produce than small things which have to be priced modestly. This is because although big items need more material they can be less labour-intensive, and it is labour that makes prices rocket. As an example, in the toymaking world it is sometimes quicker and easier to make a huge hippopotamus than a tiny toy poodle — the cutting out, stuffing and machining of the latter is fiddly and time-consuming compared with the simpler processes involved when the shape is large and easily manipulated. Intricate and complicated techniques are not good news for the craftsman unless he or she is working in the luxury end of the market where customers may be prepared to pay up to £1,000 for a bedspread or wedding dress. If you price your goods in tens of pounds rather than hundreds you simply cannot afford to be over-intricate. And even in the up-market area of interior design it makes sense to use a quick decorative skill such as fabric painting rather than a labour-intensive one like beadwork or appliqué, provided that it gives both you and your customers as much pleasure.

Costing

Most craftspeople find it very difficult to cost their product. A frequent approach to this problem is to discover — by comparing what they make with similar items being sold in good shops or craft fairs — what people are prepared to pay, then to work out:

A   how much the materials would cost, including wrapping paper, labels, etc
B   the cost of their overheads, electricity, transport, postage, etc
C   how many hours' work is involved

If the final price paid (D), minus A and B, divided by C, adds up to a reasonable hourly return for their skill, then the item is worth making. If not, something should be changed, and that could be the product; the work method; the fabric; the price, or the sales outlet, or a combination of two or more of these.

Suppose, for instance, that Lindy X is producing made-to-measure quilted, appliquéd jackets. The materials cost her £10 (A). The hours needed first to make the garment and then appliqué it add up to 15 (C). The customer will pay £30 (D). The first reaction of the inexperienced craftsman is to say, like Lindy, 'It cost me £10 and I got £30 for it so I made £20 profit.' But that is the approach that makes bank managers blanch. The £20 is not profit — it has to pay for all the overheads and for 15 hours of skilled time. If Lindy is lucky she is earning a little less than £1 an hour. She could make more money by baby-sitting.

There are various answers to the problem — quite apart from deserting the craft that she enjoys.

1   She could change her product. A jacket made from patterned fabric instead of appliquéd fabric might sell for the same price but take less hours to make. Alternatively, a simple, one-size, sleeveless tabard would be less labour-intensive than a jacket.
2   She could save time by making several jackets at once. Cutting out six jackets does not take six times as long as cutting out one jacket. Or she could boost her productivity by employing an outworker to do the straightforward work, leaving her to concentrate on the more skilled tasks.
3   She could use cheaper materials, or buy from a wholesaler at more competitive prices.
4   She could put up her price to £40 or £45 instead of £30.
5   She could change her selling outlet. With a luxury garment she could get a better price selling through an up-market shop or gallery rather than through a craft market or her own personal contacts.

Or she could change several of the variables until she arrived at a sum that seemed a reasonable return for her labour.

Suppose she put up the price of her jackets to £45 (D), managed to reduce the cost of her materials to £8.50 (A), kept her overheads constant at about £1.50 (B), and trimmed down her work method so that the number of hours she spent on each one was approximately 12 (C). Then the sum would be:

	D	£45.00
minus	A	£ 8.50
and	B	£ 1.50
equals		£35.00
divided by	C (12)	
equals		$£2^{11}/_{12}$

or an hourly return for labour of almost £3, which is more worthwhile though still underpaid.

The craftsmen I spoke to aimed to earn anything from £1.50 an hour to ten times that amount, depending upon whether they were aiming at pin money; part-time income, or full-time income. It is reasonable to expect to make £2.50 an hour but you should also aim at a profit of about 33 per cent. Suppose you were making large toys and working on a batch of several at the same time. The sum for one could be:

cost of materials	£3.00
overheads	50
time (1 hour)	2.50
sub-total	6.00
profit (33 per cent)	2.00
price charged	8.00

That might seem a good and fair price if it is to be sold by you direct to the customer, but remember that shopkeepers will double the price if they sell it for you, to pay for *their* overheads and profit margins. If you prefer to sell through retail outlets but the buyers won't pay the price you want, don't take less and do yourself down by undervaluing your time and skill — it would be better to streamline your production, simplify your product or sort out your marketing.

Keeping Books

To be business-like it is necessary to 'keep books'. Book-keeping is not a difficult task. Anyone can master it provided that it is looked upon as a regular daily or weekly task and not allowed to get out of hand. Basically, it revolves around two books — the Cash Book and the Petty Cash Book.

The Cash Book will show all your income and expenditure on a daily basis, and usually it will deal with one month's business on one double page. The date and various sources of income go on the left-hand side, the expenditure on the right, so you can see at a glance what is going on and whether your outgoings are managing to remain less than your takings. Don't panic about temporary cash-flow hiccups — if you have just bought an expensive piece of equipment or a bargain lot of fabric you will probably spend more than you earn in one month. It's only when you see that you are spending more than you are earning for several months on the run that you need worry, and perhaps make an appointment with your accountant or bank manager before you get into real financial trouble.

The easiest way to keep your Cash Book well organised is to fill in details of money received and money paid out as and when it happens. If you run into a particularly busy period and can't cope with daily entries you must keep all your bills, receipts and invoices meticulously, making sure that each one is clearly dated, ready to enter them up at the end of the month.

The Petty Cash Book should record small amounts of money paid out in cash for tiny items such as a packet of pins or a bus fare. Petty cash will be recorded as a lump sum in the Cash Book, then the lump sum broken down into detail in the Petty Cash Book, on a daily basis. Again, it is wise not to delay, or chaos could ensue!

You should also keep all your outstanding bills and demands, customers' orders and requests for information, manufacturers' notices, and so on, each one clearly dated, in an in-tray or file waiting attention. As soon as they have been dealt with a note can be written on them to remind you what action has been taken and when and then they can be filed away in folders, appropriately labelled so that they are easy to find for future reference if necessary, for your accountant in particular.

It is also helpful to have a punched file containing details of all your customers in alphabetical order, listing what they have bought, in what quantity and when, what they paid, and how promptly. This will help you to see at a glance where your best customers are, which are your fastest-selling lines, who are the problem payers and the well-behaved ones. You will also be able to check up to see if anyone who has bought a lot from you in the past has suddenly stopped ordering for no apparent reason. In cases like this it often pays dividends to chase them up and remind them of your existence and tell them about your latest ideas.

Finally, a **Contact Book** is an invaluable asset. In this you put the names, addresses, telephone numbers and details of anyone you might find useful or need to contact in the future. They may be retail outlets which have been recommended to you; other craftspeople you would like to meet; organisers of trade fairs or craft markets; sources of material, trimmings, labels; colleges or summer schools offering specialist training, and so on. Enter them alphabetically by group rather than by individual, eg Craftspeople, Fairs, Manufacturers, Summer Schools, and always leave room for expansion — a loose-leaf file is ideal — because you will find that you get more and more contacts as time goes by.

As well as being careful about getting your initial buying and costing right; keeping your books efficiently, and keeping tabs on your customers and contacts, good organisation also means being sensible about the way you use your time.

Saving Time

Though buying fabrics and materials is an important part of your work it should be done methodically so that it doesn't take up hours that could be used producing the goods. Experienced business craftspeople tend to limit their buying days to no more than one or two a month. Similarly, you should not spend a disproportionate amount of time selling rather than making. The equivalent of one or two days a week should be ample once you have got yourself established and your work is known because then, with luck, the crafts will sell themselves for the main part and repeat orders and recommendations will make up the bulk of your sales.

The important thing is to plan ahead and to use time intelligently. You should know in the spring what you will be selling in the autumn and have laid your plans, especially for the busy approach to Christmas. You should use your quiet periods to stock up for the busy ones, working steadily whether or not the orders are there. And you should always stick to deadlines. If you promise delivery three weeks after the order is received, three weeks it must be. If you can't cope change the delivery date to four or six weeks after ordering. In my experience customers don't mind waiting if they know they're going to wait. What causes ill feelings and cancelled orders are broken promises and unexpected delays.

To run a freelance business takes a lot of self-discipline, hard work and courage. You have to keep going when customers seem totally uninterested. You have to keep working when you are tired and over-stretched. You have to be sufficiently self-confident to offer your goods for sale at a realistic price even in the face of buyers who will try to beat you down. And you have to maintain, even when you are exhausted with over-work or dispirited by lack of it, immaculate books and records and impeccable organisational practices. The good thing is that it gets easier as you accustom yourself to it. What's more, the business of wearing three hats at once — those of moneyman, salesman and craftsman — means that life is never, ever, dull.

9 Presentation

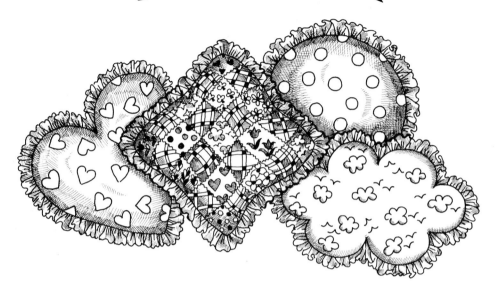

It is very obvious that if they are to give pleasure, and consequently find a market, the crafts you create must look good. The good looks must come first of all from the products themselves — from their cut, colour, design, quality of fabric and craftsmanship. That is self-evident. But they must also come from the way in which they are presented.

Labelling

To start with, most fabric crafts aimed at the commercial market should be labelled. It is very attractive to have your own personal label because this gives an item your own individual stamp, and goes on advertising it for you after the purchase has been made. Fabric labels can be bought from several manufacturers, some of whom give advice as to what information should be included. Be careful to choose one which will supply in hundreds rather than thousands unless you are making vast quantities. Diverse Marketing, Westruther, Gordon, Berwickshire TD3 6NE are recommended since they not only do name labels but also size, fibre content and wash-care labels, and swing tickets, packaging

and rubber stamps. Send a stamp for their catalogue and samples. Other label suppliers are listed in Appendix 6.

Note that occasionally, if you sell to retail shops, they will want *their* labels on your goods. If so, they will tell you about this when they place their order and either provide you with a supply of their own labels or ask you to organise this for them. If they do the latter, make sure you include the extra expense in your costing.

The first function of a label is to be your trademark — but there are others. For instance, you may want to emphasise that your goods are 'Hand-crafted in the UK' since there is a special interest both in hand-made goods and British-made goods, and some prestige stores are keen to buy British to sell to tourist customers looking for something which represents British craftsmanship at its best. If you are making clothes for retail outlets you will also need to put a size label on garments — this may a simple S, M or L, or a more specific 10, 12, 14 or 16, etc. For children's wear it's usual to put the age of the child for whom it is intended.

Local authorities are now very anxious to enforce the EEC regulations which insist that textile products should be labelled with details of the composition of the material used — 50 per cent cotton, 50 per cent polyester, or 100 per cent new wool, as the case may be; and if the goods are padded or filled, that also has to appear on the fibre content label. So, a cushion might carry the information:

Cover — 100% cotton
Filling — 100% polyester
Hand made in Wales
by
CLOUD CUCKOO

There is a British Standard (BS 1425) covering the fillings and stuffings for bedding, toys, upholstery and other domestic articles, and you can look at this in the public library. It is advisable to conform to it, and to state on your label that you have conformed, since it reassures the customer and is sound selling policy. Another British Standard (BS 2747) is a textile care labelling code which uses symbols devised by the Home Laundering Consultative Council. It is helpful at least to label your product with 'Dry Clean Only', 'Hand Wash' or 'Machine Washable'. Many craftspeople told me that they used labels to give specific care instructions not only to prevent themselves from the wrath of irate customers should things go wrong in the wash, but also to prevent their customers from disappointment should they inadvertently damage something they had chosen with love and care. If in any doubt at all about machine washing advise hand washing. The customer may ignore you and try it in the machine; if it works she'll be delighted. But if it doesn't, it's not your fault.

The result of all this is that, depending upon what you make, you may end up with as many as three labels on your craft item. One will give your name, telephone number and/or address, and something like 'Hand made in the UK'. One will give the size. And one will give fibre content and laundry instructions. Alternatively, you may combine the same information in various other ways. A good label-maker will advise you on this.

You have to be careful if you export your products — and even small-scale crafts businesses often do at least occasional exports — since all

DESIGNED AND
HAND EMBROIDERED
BY MARGARET GRANGER

MADE BY

Carpet Bags

ROUGHAM,
SUFFOLK, ENGLAND.

HILLSIDE CRAFTS

25, Castle Drive
Kendal, Cumbria LA9 7BJ
Phone: (0539) 23769

Batik & Screen Printed Clothes
Shoes & Papercraft
Designed by Lene Bragger

countries have their own rules and regulations about textile labelling. If you receive an order from abroad, perhaps as a result of selling from a craft fair or market, make sure that you ask about this aspect, and if your own labels won't stand up to the laws of the importing country suggest that the buyer should either provide you with labels or bear the extra cost you will incur by having them specially made.

Packaging

To keep your product in pristine condition but clearly visible you may decide to pack them into polythene bags which are available in all shapes and sizes from a multitude of sources. The problem is not finding a supplier — there are dozens listed under 'Packaging' in the *Yellow Pages* of the telephone directory. The difficulty lies in finding a supplier who doesn't necessarily think you should buy about ten thousand bags at a time! Most craftspeople have to go through the dreary business of telephoning about a dozen possible sources before they find the right one, but with patience the right one *is* eventually found.

It is worth investing in polythene bags since they can save you pounds if there is any danger of your goods getting soiled or faded or damaged while on display. When I was buying for my shop there were some things that I would only buy if they were protected by transparent packaging because I knew the nervous strain of trying to keep them clean and untouched by sticky fingers would not be worth any profit I might make. And this is even more important if the contract between the craftsman and shop is on a sale-or-return basis. Not even the most diligent and careful of shopkeepers can guarantee that all his or her stock will remain in perfect condition if it is left unprotected.

You may also like to buy paper bags and carrier bags with your logo, name, address and telephone number printed on them. This is expensive the first time you do it since it is necessary to have a special block made for printing, as a rule. However, the price drops when you reorder once you have made that initial investment. Your own printed paperware also gives a thoroughly professional look to your operation which tends to impress customers much more than scratting around for used bags and creased wrapping paper. Jane Playford, the lacemaker, told me that it had taken her a long time to face up to the idea of spending £300 for ten thousand bags in two sizes, but she had never regretted one penny of it. In fact she wished she had done it sooner and was looking forward to having her own printed carrier bags as soon as her bank balance would stand it.

Finally, for the ultimate touch of luxury, a few packs of tissue paper for wrapping makes an attractive finish. Bottle wrap is the cheapest and comes in many lovely colours as well as white, but be warned. The colour can run and cause staining, so it's necessary to take great care to

avoid it getting wet. Some packaging suppliers are listed in Appendix 6.

Needless to say, it is imperative to add the cost of packaging to the cost of other materials, or overheads, when you are calculating the selling price for your goods, though the amount spent *per item* may be minimal.

Display

With this sort of attention to detail everything you sell will look good, fresh and immaculate when handed over to the buyer. But another aspect of presentation is display. This depends not only upon what you sell, but also on how you sell it. If you sell from a stall in a market or craft fair the stall itself must be attractively 'dressed' — perhaps covered with neutrally coloured hessian or swathes of cloth which will enhance rather than detract from the colours of your goods. The items themselves should be well set out on various levels. You may decide to build up a display with covered boxes and hang drapery, goods or photographs at the back or round the edges. At all costs avoid the jumble sale look. Artistically arranged masses, mounds and piles of beautiful, colourful crafts can look irresistible, but the same objects, spread out at random on one level with little thought for creating a pleasing picture, are not likely to attract attention. Remember that window-dressing is a skill for which people train, so learn the tricks of the trade by watching how the professionals do it, and put them to good use.

If you are selling through party plan, once again the general appearance — with goods displayed at all levels, careful attention to colour, texture and variety, plenty of space allowed for people to move, and look, and feel — is vital. For clothes, one or two tailor's dummies give three-dimensional appeal, and whatever you are selling, it often pays dividends to have a folding display board with drawings, photographs, fabric patterns and promotional material.

If you sell to retail outlets it is more difficult to win the right to have any say in how your goods are shown off, but it is worth at least trying to explain to the shop owner, with immense tact and diplomacy, that:

> a large selection always sells better than just two or three items (when I ran my craft shop it was amazing how often I bought about twenty articles from a craftsman, sold the first eighteen like hot cakes, and then couldn't move the last two until I restocked, no matter how carefully I displayed them. This is very common. It seems that customers have more confidence if they have a lot to choose from — two or three seem like unwanted left-overs)
> nothing sells well if tucked away on bottom shelves or in badly lit and inaccessible corners, which could be better used for storing goods with which to replenish emptying spaces rather than for display
> nothing sells well, except perhaps at sale prices, if

it begins to look grubby and tatty, so items made from materials like fur fabric should be brushed regularly to retain their glow and texture
cushion covers only attract the eye if at least some of them have cushion pads inside. A pretty pile of plump cushions spilling out of a wicker hamper acts like a magnet. The same pile of cushion covers, neatly folded and stacked on a low shelf, will hardly be noticed

It is important to get your goods well displayed whether you are selling them on a straight business deal or doing a sale-or-return transaction, because if they don't move quickly you will either find that there is no repeat order or that you will get them all returned, looking a little bit sad and sorry for themselves, three to six months later. Single-handed shopkeepers often find it difficult to find time for display, but personally, I was always delighted if a craftsman offered to do his or her own display for me, provided that we had an initial discussion about the amount of space to be used and the most suitable place to site it. You could always make a tentative offer to do this and see what sort of reaction you get. If a shop simply refuses to show off your goods to their best advantage you should think twice about selling through that particular outlet.

Effective packaging and display are essential to good marketing, which depends largely on presentation for its success. But the most important part of presentation is the way you present yourself and your goods to your customer — whether he or she is a high-powered super-store buyer or a casual Saturday morning shopper. If you have a genuine pride and pleasure in what you have to offer, and if you take an obvious interest in the person to whom you are trying to sell; if your manner is courteous and friendly, and you show both an enthusiasm for what you make and an understanding of what the customer requires; then you are already halfway there. Presumably you belong to the world of crafts because it is a world of pleasure and beauty — there are, after all, easier ways of earning money. So let that pleasure and beauty permeate your business dealings, and the chances are, they will turn them into a profitable enterprise.

10 Craftsmen Talking

JANE PLAYFORD
Lacemaker
'Jane's Pincushion'

I've done embroidery all my life — well, ever since I was three. I had a sickly childhood so I couldn't do anything very active, and the embroidery kept me busy. My mother's a very gifted needlewoman, and an artist as well. Design work is her thing. She taught me almost everything I know. I went to college to train as a teacher but not in needlecrafts — but I didn't need that because she taught me so much, and still does. We forget we're mother and daughter — it's teacher and student. We both teach now, between us we do classes in upholstery, tapestry, embroidery, lamp-shade making and soft-furnishing, as well as my lacemaking.

I started making lace in 1978 because it was cheaper than embroidery. I used to get through embroidery kits so quickly it was costing a fortune. I began to go to classes for the lace but I didn't get on very well there so I taught myself from a book. At that time I was going to Belgium about once a month — I have relatives there, and lots of friends, and I go often so I'm well acquainted with Bruges lace. I used to go and look at the lace, in museums and places like that, and watch it being made, and *learn.* It was mainly Belgian flower work there, but now I do all sorts of lace — torchon, Bedfordshire, Buckinghamshire . . .

I started making lace and selling supplies, making it into a proper business, two years ago, with £500 I raised by selling my boat because I didn't want to borrow from the bank. Now I've managed to buy a lovely new car, and the next thing I have in mind is a pony. I never for one moment thought that I'd earn enough for a decent car in two years! You can't make a living from lacemaking alone, though, so I began to sell lacemaking equipment by postal service, running the business from my home. I still do that, in the evenings mostly. I sell equipment all over the world — to Finland, Australia, Iceland, Saudi Arabia. Lacemaking is thriving all over the world. I even sell to Belgium, which pleases me. I knew before I started that there would be a demand for the service because I used to find it so difficult to get equipment for my own needs.

Now I make a good living by combining teaching, running an advisory service, demonstrating, making lace, and selling it, along with all the other things that are needed by people who are interested in a whole range of needlecrafts. A year ago a crafts centre was opened near where I live, at Wroxham, Norfolk. 'Wroxham Barns', it's called, because it's a group of old barns, beautifully converted. It's a combination of workshops where craftsmen can work, demonstrate and sell their wares; a big gallery and shop; a restaurant; and picnic areas, walks and an adventure play-ground, too. I was approached and asked if I would take over one of the workshops. I agreed to take over one of the units on two understandings. It shouldn't be just for lace, it should sell embroidery, too, articles *and* equipment. And my husband, Mike, should have a workshop, too, if possible. Mike is a woodturner and, among other things, he makes beautiful lace bobbins. He started making them for me, mainly because I was fed up with using plastic ones. Now we sell lots of them, both in the Barns and through mail order. There are lots of different types, many of them from exotic woods. And some of them are hand-painted by my mother. As a souvenir she paints the workshop's name — Jane's Pincushion — on some of them, then a tiny picture of a hedgehog — the hedgehog is our symbol because it's a sort of pincushion! Both ideas were agreed to and we moved into the Barns in February, 1984.

It's worked out very well. I'm delighted. I can make lace in the workshop, and sell it, advise people and help them, all at the same time. I don't waste any of my day, not a moment. The sort of things I make are collars, pendants and brooches, lace pictures, edgings and decorative pieces for cushions, pincushions, and handkerchiefs, and lace insets for paperweights, brushes, boxes, dusting bowls, fan-sticks, trays and mirrors. I sell kits of these things for people to make up themselves. At present I'm working on a pink lace rose for a wedding hat, and I do primroses, too. There are lots of advantages in working in a crafts centre like this one. To start with, our accommodation is excellent but our rents are very reasonable. A lot of advertising is done for us — we've been taken up by the Tourist Board, so thousands of people come, and we're just about guaranteed a steady flow of customers and visitors — people who wouldn't bother to search the workshops out anywhere else, but come because it's *there.* I do a lot of advertising on my own account — a great deal in 'crafty' magazines like *Popular Crafts* and *Leisure and Crafts,* which is a new one. I belong to the Lace Guild of England, but only occasionally advertise in their magazine because I prefer to aim for the more popular end of the market. Membership of the Lace Guild is a prestige thing really, and it acts as a centre of information and source of material. They're hoping to get premises soon that are big enough and central enough to bring everything together under one roof. It is very important to get oneself known, and press write-ups and things like that are very useful. I was lucky. I belong to the Norfolk Lacemakers, and we meet in Norwich monthly. We have Lace Days where we can lay out our supplies if asked to attend, and people come to buy and listen to talks and watch demonstrations. Someone saw me at one of these and was interested in my supplies, and after that I was invited to Lace Days all over the country and got quite well known.

The other thing that helped me, funnily enough, was the fact that Mike served in the Falklands, with the Navy. When he went away I didn't sit around and mope. I thought, 'I'll have to look to the future, plan ahead, work out what I'm going to do whether he comes home or whether he doesn't.' So I worked terribly hard. It was the only way I could cope. People rallied round and supported me — the 'brave little wife', I suppose — and my business improved in the six months he was away.

I am a hard worker naturally, though — I have to be. I'm at the Barns five-and-a-half days a week, I teach most evenings, and I do up my postal orders at night. It's a fourteen-hour day, and a seven-day week in high season. But it's not so much a job as a way of life — because the whole family is in it together. I'd say it's really a family pulling together. Mike's there just two doors away, and my mother and I sometimes demonstrate here together. We sometimes make things together, too. The latest, which is on sale in the craft gallery, is a lovely cushion that combines all our crafts — a damask centre embroidered with cross-stitch, trimmed with lace, mounted on moiré, and then the whole thing finished with a hand-ruched moiré edging. My father is involved, too. He makes lacemaking pillow-stands — both free-standing and Belgian, similar to the ones they use in the Belgian lacemaking schools. And we all share a house and help each other. I don't think I could manage otherwise.

Lacemaking is a good craft to take up because you don't need a lot of equipment to get started. I make up a Starter's Kit myself. That includes: a lace pillow, stuffed with polystyrene (traditionally they should be stuffed with barley straw); thirty plastic bobbins (you can go on to wooden ones, which are more expensive but more beautiful, once you get going); a big reel of thread; wire and beads, to put spangles on the ends of the bobbins, to give weight and help tension; a pricking card, to make the pattern on; and a set of instructions. That's all you need to begin. And a lot of patience. It won't make your living for you but it can be a pleasant and profitable hobby.

ANNA POTTEN
Textile Worker

I left school at 16 and went to the Art Department in a technical college as it was called then to do my A-levels and special art. From there I went to Leicester Poly to do a BA Honours Degree in Printed Textiles. I am dyslexic, and in some ways this has been a positive advantage to me. All my tutors were very good, helpful and supportive, because I had a recognisable problem. They weren't as sympathetic to other students who might just be finding the course too difficult to cope with, or couldn't keep up with the work. The dyslexia has also affected my perception as an artist. Before I could read well — up until I was 13 — I perceived a lot of words as areas of colour, shapes and blocks. Even now I'm more struck by shapes than words, and I've realised that writing letters is really drawing shapes. You draw a circle for an 'O', a triangle with a bar for an 'A'. I see things in two dimensions — it's much more difficult for me to work in three dimensions, though that's what I do now for a lot of the time. My handicap has made me more conscious of what exactly people look at. I always knew I wanted to be an artist but if I hadn't had this problem people would have tried to channel me into some other direction, more academic or practical. As it was they always said wasn't it lucky that at least I could do art.

My first job was in a costume museum, but while I was working there I decided that what I'd like to do was go to Botswana with Voluntary Service Overseas and set up a textile project. Then suddenly I was offered studio space in an arts centre and it seemed like a good idea, too good to turn down. Eileen, a girl I was at college with, teamed up with me and we worked together making clothes — not because we particularly wanted to but to make money. I made the fabrics, she made the clothes. She'd been working with Zandra Rhodes. That didn't work out very well. The things we made were slightly removed from what people wanted, and it was a big problem having to put such a lot of time into selling instead of making. So, we decided to do what we *wanted*. Eileen made patchwork and I created fabric, and since it's not easy to sell bits

of fabric on its own I made them up into cushion covers. When I got used to working to a 12-inch square I found it very satisfying. It's so small that it's a useful constraint. I worked from my own drawings, based on my local landscape, Salisbury Plain — lots of fields, not many trees. I embroidered them, and did beadwork, and appliqué, lifting the pattern with stitching. I experimented with shape and colour. A lot of black and white shapes merged together and gradually became a herd of cows. I liked that and cows were the main motif of my first show. They weren't just cushions, they were embroidered landscapes. I made scarves, too, from batik. And printed woollen scarves, very fine wool, embroidered with a line of stitching around the edge.

I tried to pay myself £2 an hour but it was very difficult. I sold from the studio, and through craft shows, and to shops. Arts centres are good places to sell from because they have lots of art and craft exhibitions. Sometimes I'd make the first approach and offer my work to an arts centre — sometimes they'd approach me because they'd seen my work and invite me to show. Once you get on to the arts centre circuit you could go on and on for ever if you wanted to. I got a lot of commissions, too. That was nice because I knew that I was making things that people felt were very special, really valued. Much nicer than selling to shops when they could have afforded to pay me ten times as much as they did. The commission thing is like a roller coaster — you go on selling to the same customers. They'd bring wallpaper and paint for me to match up with a cushion, and then I'd get asked to do the curtains as well. I began to get uncomfortable about it, though. I'm very involved in several social issues and I felt that that side of my life didn't marry with selling expensive luxury goods, so I had to move on from there.

The change of direction really started when I was asked to help make a banner for a festival and I felt — this is more exciting, there are more people involved, it's more important. So now I'm a freelance community artist, helping people to make things for their own events or celebrations. I'm very interested in working with women's groups. A lot of women undervalue themselves and think they have no skills. But they do have skills in sewing and knitting. Once they see that those are important they begin to value themselves more and build up their confidence. I've been involved in all sorts of textile projects — helping to make a huge sheep, for instance, for Wilton Fair. And for the Newbury Festival we made kites — very nice, though I say it myself. A bit like butterflies. They flap . . . very slightly. We did one big one, 6ft by 2ft, which we made to hang under the roof of Newbury Arts Centre, and it looked lovely — *and* it was aerodynamically sound. The little kites, made in the same delta shape, sold really well.

The problem about being a freelance is that one works in fits and starts. There's never enough money to pay community artists, and we need more funding from the government for a whole range of projects, but I don't see that

happening. I still do some of my other sort of work as well. I like working for exhibitions, having a definite goal to work towards. That's a good discipline. Commissions, too. I was asked to make curtains with poppies on and I enjoyed that. I'm into house decoration now — I made some curtains from raw silk and they were beautiful. I make things for people if they ask me but I'm not interested any longer in touting things around. I've done my share of that. I like to investigate new ideas — fastening cushion covers with ties instead of zips, for instance. I made some like that and the shopkeepers and gallery owners all said they liked them but they wouldn't buy them. It was very frustrating. The more inventive I was the less I was likely to sell. I was in a cul-de-sac. For me it's more exciting working with people, developing and sharing skills, making beautiful things together.

JUDY MORE
Dressmaker

I got a First in Philosophy, but as my father said, 'Philosophy's OK but what about the bread?' He was right, but I didn't care. Most of my working life I've earned money by sewing. I've been able to make my own clothes since I was 12 years old so I suppose it was quite natural that I should be wardrobe mistress for our amateur theatre group when I was at college in South Carolina. After that I moved on to San Francisco and got into professional theatre, starting at the bottom as a jobbing seamstress.

In 1970 I came to Britain to visit a friend, an English girl. As I staggered off the plane, after about twenty-four hours in transit, Amanda greeted me with, 'I have this wonderful idea about how we can make our fortune — toymaking!' So, we made up lots of toys, hand-puppets, huge velvet animals in gorgeous colours, and went sallying out to the shops to try to sell them. We tried all the places that seemed likely, Chelsea boutiques, and those up at Hampstead — both of us sharing the business of making *and* selling. That was the idea, but the way it turned out there was a lot of making and not much

selling. That's when we discovered the difficulty of making things commercially. The toys the shops liked they wanted *tomorrow*, and two dozen, please. There was no way we could do that. The toys we *could* mass produce in a hurry were small and simple, quite ordinary, I suppose, and those the shops were just not interested in. I think we just about broke even in the end.

So, I went back into the theatre, first at Leatherhead, and then at the National Youth Theatre in London. I had very good facilities for dyeing fabrics there, so in my spare time I used to buy canvas and make men's trousers to order, in any colour they fancied.

You name it, I've made it. Baby clothes, quilted nappy bags that double as changing mats, maternity clothes, loose covers, *millions* of curtains. I come from a long line of curtain-makers. All the time I worked in the theatre people asked me to make them things, so it's always brought me in a second income. Like trousers for tall women. Every tall woman I have ever known has asked me to make trousers for her, I'm not kidding. I've always made my own clothes and people see what I'm wearing and ask me to make something like that for them. And I sew for shops as well, especially baby clothes. I just asked if they'd be interested in selling some of my things and they said yes. Baby clothes are nice to make because the sewing is easy and the embroidery is interesting. I design the clothes myself but use transfers for the embroidery. Then perhaps I'll personalise it by working in the child's initial or something like that.

I've never relied on making things as my sole income but I've always made extra money that way, apart from the toymaking fiasco, and *that* taught me a lesson that was worth paying for! Now my first job is to look after my children who are 4½ and 2 years old so sewing brings me jn a bit of money that is my own, something for myself. Fixing prices is really very difficult. Usually I charge what the market will wear, that's the best guideline. If I'm sewing for a shop they tell me what they can get from the customer and I have to get my charge down to about half of that so I have to figure out how long it will take me, what's the quickest way of doing it, whether it's worth it. There's no point in working long hours for a few pence — usually I've managed to avoid working for nothing.

I have plans to develop the sewing when the children are at school and I can have a good crack at *time*. More children's clothes, and maternity clothes. Particularly maternity clothes. One thing I've learnt, before you go into anything you have to judge the market, and, do you know, I've never ever talked to a mother who's been totally satisfied with the choice of maternity clothes she's offered in the shops. So that will be my line. You *can* make money if you think your way through.

SUZY Q

CHILDRENS WEAR

152 WOODLAND DRIVE,
WATFORD.
HERTS. WD1 3OB.
TEL: WATFORD (0923) 48526.

SUE MANNERS
Children's Clothes
Suzy Q'

I make and sell highly individual children's wear — my own designs, very original, good quality, and quite different from anything you'd find in the shops. I do clothes for both boys and girls, for the 2- to 10-year-old range.

I sell through parties — the party-plan method. Friends, or friends of friends, sometimes people who've bought my clothes in the past, or been to a SUZY Q party, organise parties for me in their homes and invite people they know who might be interested — young mothers mostly, with small children. I make up samples of my current collection — I have two collections a year, one for the autumn into winter, and one for the spring into summer — and I take them along to show to people. They can order the style they like in any size and in any of the fabrics in my range. I take a fabric sample card to show them, and measure up the children at the party if they've brought them along. Otherwise they give me their exact measurements.

They have the clothes within three to four weeks of placing the order. I need one week to do the cutting — most of which my husband does while I pack it up to go to my outworkers — then one week for the making up to be done by the outworkers, and one week for the garment to come back to me for checking and packing up and returning to the party hostess. Usually my customers pick up the goods from the lady who organised the party in the first place. The hostess gets 10 per cent of the value of the orders I receive, in clothes. Or, if I do an event for a charity, the charity gets that 10 per cent in cash for its funds.

Originally, I trained as a secretary but my hobby has always been dressmaking. After I got married I saw a two-year course of evening classes being offered at the local college. It was called 'Design and Make Your Own Clothes' and it gave me an insight into design and basic pattern-cutting. I enjoyed that very much but when it was over at first I didn't really use the training to the full advantage. I just mucked about, making my own patterns. When my daughter was born I started making things for her and I found that she'd wear a dress and other people would see her in it and say they'd like one like that for their little girl. When she was 18 months old my next-door neighbour and I got chatting — we were both short of money, you know how it is when you have a young family — and she said we should get together on this. She'd do the organising and I could do the sewing. We decided to have a go, almost jokingly at first. I'm a great collector of materials so I had masses of stuff to make clothes from. I made them up, she invited people along to see them, and they bought them. It all started from there, but after a while my neighbour moved away and I decided to set myself up in business properly. That was about two years ago.

It was hard work in the beginning, getting started. My friends rallied round to help me get going. Now it's easier. I've got used to selling on a party basis. Really, the clothes sell themselves — I would never push them. I'd never try to persuade people to buy. Quite apart from the fact that I just couldn't bring myself to do it, I don't think it's good psychology. I'd rather women came and saw my clothes and just liked them so much that they wanted to have them for their children. And that's what happens, especially with the dresses, which are my best sellers. Sometimes a child will be brought to one of the parties wearing something I've made and people will say, 'Isn't that lovely? Doesn't it look beautiful! Aren't you clever!' And, or course, that's great. I must admit I enjoy the praise, enjoy other people's pleasure in what I've made. It makes it all worth it.

It is a lot of work. Sometimes it gets on top of me. It can be a slog, but basically I enjoy it, especially designing. Designing is the big joy — I'd do that all the time if I could. All this organising isn't my sort of thing really, but I can do it now because I've had to. You have to be business-like.

I design a new collection twice a year. I start work on my summer range straight after Christmas, and I start selling the clothes in March and on until July. Then I have my summer break. In August I start working on my winter fabrics. That's really hard, having to work in August, but it's got to be done because I start selling again in mid-September and go on till Christmas.

I buy my fabrics wholesale at a trade fair held twice a year, and I follow up some of the advertisements in the *Drapers Record*. That's the trade magazine which is absolutely essential reading for anyone in the clothes business. When I started I used to buy fabrics from Brick Lane in the East End of London, the place where the market traders buy. Manufacturers' off-cuts, and oddments, and remaindered lines are sold there. But now the materials I use must be of good quality. I must have some come-back if anything goes wrong, if it is flawed, or doesn't wash properly. I can't afford to take risks or turn out anything shoddy, so I have to be able to say to the manufacturer, 'This isn't good enough!' if I have any complaints.

I try to fix my charges very carefully. I would say that my prices are moderate, the same sort of range as Marks & Spencer's. It is possible to buy things cheaper but you'd pay a lot more at a boutique. And, of course, mine are made to measure. I work out my costs as carefully as possible. I add together the materials and all the bits and pieces, and the wages I pay my outworkers, and the final price is based on this plus a reasonable profit margin. I'm most meticulous about keeping records — that's very important. My husband's very involved. He funded me to get me started and he does the books. We have an accountant, too. We needed him to advise us about the most effective way of arranging our finances, and he claims back VAT for us. Children's clothes are zero-rated so we can get back the VAT we have paid on goods or equipment.

At present I have ten outworkers but the

number varies considerably. I advertise for them in the first place, in the local paper. They ring me up and we have an initial telephone conversation; then, if they are still interested, I go to see them, take samples of work and materials, and discuss prices. Then I leave a piece of work for them to do. Usually it would be a shirt, that's the best thing. If they do that well we go on from there. I pay them fair piece-rates based on a reasonable hourly payment. I wouldn't pay them a pittance. I work out how long it should take an experienced worker to make a particular garment and base the fee on that. Once a week I take them materials and collect what they have made since my last visit. I don't have many problems with them. Most of the girls have young children. If one of the children is ill and the work is likely to be delayed they must ring and let me know. Sometimes I can give them extra time. If not, I collect their work and take it to one of the others.

I enjoy SUZY Q very much but it really is hard work; it's not as easy as it sounds. And there are snags. I sometimes have to work when I'd rather not, like during the summer holidays. And sometimes an outworker might drop out, just on the spur of the moment, and I'm left in the lurch with a lot of orders. A month before Christmas I lost three outworkers for no particular reason.

Some of them just do it for a couple of seasons and then get fed up with it, but I do like to keep them for longer than that if possible. When they pack up without warning I find I have to do a lot of the sewing myself on top of everything else, and if it happens just before Christmas it can cause chaos because that's my busiest time. I end up working until the early hours of the morning. The other difficulty I get, very occasionally, is people cancelling their orders at the last minute. I don't mind if they cancel quickly, within a day or two, but if a garment has been made to measure and it's suddenly left on your hands it can be a dead loss financially. I'm considering getting round that one by asking for a deposit with the order. Some customers need time to save up to pay the full bill but if they put down a little bit when they order it shows that they really are serious about it.

But the pleasures, and the profits, far outweigh the problems. The number of orders is very encouraging at present. My children are still little so I can only work part-time just now, but eventually I'd like to expand. I *say* I'd like to be the Tupperware of children's clothes, but not really. It would be nice, though, to get so much bigger and better that my husband could leave his job and we could work together on a full-time basis. He would like that and so would I.

HARRICK HART
Bagmaker
'Carpet Bags'

Carpet Bags started almost by chance nine years ago. My partner, Loretta Quartey, and I were co-founders of an ecology society called 'Green Deserts', and we wanted to raise some money for it by taking a stall at Bungay May Fair. We couldn't think what to make to sell from the stall and then we thought — carpet bags, what else! We were very much into luggage since at that time we were both active film-makers, always on the move, all over the world, and we needed the right sort of bag to cart our belongings around. We used to use canvas bags, made by a friend of

ours, with lots of little pockets and compartments in them, ideal for travelling. Then she stopped making them and we couldn't find anything as good so we decided to make some for ourselves. The idea of using old carpets as our material appealed to us because we like the thought of recycling, using up things that would otherwise be thrown away, giving them a second useful life. That's very satisfying. And we knew that it was extremely tough as well as being beautiful and colourful. Besides which, we could get hold of it for nothing, or next to nothing. People are only too glad to get *rid* of old carpets.

We made a dozen bags for Bungay Fair. 'Cosmic Bags' we called them. They had a leather double-strap handle and could be used

GEOFF'S HOUSE   ROUGHAM   BURY ST. EDMUNDS   SUFFOLK IP30 9LY
Phone: BEYTON (0359) 70825

in lots of different ways — over the shoulder, hand-held, open and easily accessible or safely locked to stow away in the hold of an aeroplane, huge and capacious, or folded over so that they became quite small — just the sort of bag we needed ourselves and resilient enough to last a lifetime and more. We took them to Bungay Fair — and sold none, not one! So, we got straight in the car and went to London and sold half of them to Harrods and half to Liberty's. Both the buyers took one look, said 'Aren't they lovely?', and took some. Since then we've never looked back. On two occasions we've been the largest selling item in Liberty's leather department — though in fact we use very little leather. And we sell through lots of other outlets, the General Trading Company, Naturally British in Covent Garden, shops, galleries and craft centres all over the country. Export orders to the United States, too. We got a mention in *Vogue* magazine and as a result of that, people found us, and got in touch, and we made American contacts. That was very useful, the *Vogue* publicity. Much better than advertising. We've only advertised once; we paid for three weeks' worth in *Time Out*. It cost us £70 and we took £70, so we didn't lose money but it certainly wasn't a successful selling exercise.

The most lucrative thing to get into is the mail-order catalogues — then you're selling in hundreds instead of dozens. We've been in Liberty's Christmas catalogue for three years running, and we're in the Country Garden catalogues, too. Though we're a cottage industry in Suffolk, functioning from quite primitive premises on old machines, and with no formal training, we've sold more than ten thousand bags now, each one hand-crafted, individual and unique. We do work hard at the selling and the public relations — keep our customers informed of our new lines, and make a real effort over our brochures and advertising material, which must look really good.

Loretta is the designing talent. She designs the bags, almost all of them, and our lovely logo is her work. We keep adding new types of bags — the Town Bag is our most recent, we launched that with its own special hand-out — and we're working on new prototypes all the time. After the Cosmic Bag, for globe-trotters, we added the Gladstone Bag, the Roller Bag, the Slouch Pouch, the Round Duffle, the Clutch, Pocket Pouch, Shoulder Bag and Neck Purse. We've got a big, slim Brief Bag, too — much nicer than a leather brief-case. That didn't go too well at first, but it's beginning to catch on now. Currently we're spending a lot of time thinking how to make men's bags that they won't mind carrying. Using darker, plainer colours. And I'm playing around with one made from car-upholstery fabric. There could be a market for co-ordinating car-bags! We've just launched two new product lines: Oriental carpet bags made from very special hand-made Eastern carpets, Baluchi, Samarkand, Sirvan, Afghan, etc, most beautiful and very expensive and exclusive; and our Quartey range of tapestry bags, made from new tapestry material in traditional designs, with a special interlining to give it incredible strength, while still remaining lightweight. We want all our bags to be really tough and long-lasting,

Carpet Bags

Unique Carpet Bags made in our studios in Suffolk, England, with the care, craftsmanship and quality that are rare these days. Each bag is different, created from an almost infinite variety of pattern, colour and texture inherent in carpets. With our special treatment of double washing with pure soap, the selected pieces of old carpet maintain their strength whilst becoming beautifully soft.

The Unlined Shoulder Bag
With strap of matching carpet this rounded bag is strong - made for hard wear - yet with good looks from every aspect

The Gladstone Bag
A traditional Carpet Bag, with a large capacity, of universal appeal. Fully lined with hardwearing polyester cotton. The substantial frame on this bag has an antique brass finish, a joy-to-handle carpet handle, and with lock and key this bag will go far.

The Slouch Pouch
Gently curving lines enhance the floral designs of this already pretty bag with its hip-length cord and velcro fastening.

The Lined Shoulder Bag
Fully lined with polyester cotton fabric, matching strap, and a lovely overlocked stitch finish on all edges. This rectangular bag suits both casual and formal occasions with ease.

The Roller Bag
The roller bag combines practicality with good looks. Easily carried over the shoulder as well as in the hand. Soft, round and spacious, this bag has a chunky 20" nylon zip for ease of closing.

Carpet bags from Carpet Bags combine their timeless classic style with the soft richness and distinctive patterns only found in genuine quality carpet, proving their wide ranging appeal. From exclusive west end London stores - where they have been selling since spring 1974 - through to town shops and country fairs, Carpet Bags have proved immensely attractive.

The Clutch Bag
A graceful accessory for evening and daytime. Soft to touch with carefully selected patterns. Useful capacity with smooth complimentary lining.

The Round Duffle
This versatile, lightweight, unlined bouncy bag has a padded bottom. The strap is single solid leather which carries well in the hand, will clip to the base for wearing over the shoulder, plus many other configurations.

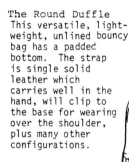

The Pocket Pouch
With short strong cord strap to wear securely underarm. Easy access velcro fastening, ideal for passports, cheque books, purses.

The Cosmic Bag
This resilient bag is made to last a lifetime or more. The solid leather double strap handle has multiple modes of use, from single for over the shoulder, to quadruple for in the hand. Heavy duty eyelets and smooth yet hardwearing loose polyester cotton lining. Double stitched seams and triple stitched corners.

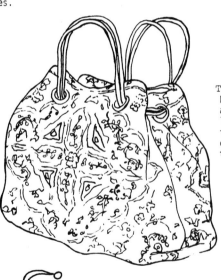

The Neck Purse
Fun, popular, and a great little present for everyone, especially the young.

CARE OF YOUR CARPET BAG
If your Carpet Bag should get wet, dry well. Clean with soap and water. When using cleaning fluids test a discreet area first. Brush well to raise the pile.

ROUGHAM, BURY ST EDMUNDS, SUFFOLK, ENGLAND

thoroughly practicable. Using tapestry will make us more viable, for several reasons. Since the material is always easily available, in the same colours and patterns and quality, there's no difficulty in fulfilling specific orders, and there's no labour involved in getting it and preparing it for use, the way there is with old carpeting. It takes an enormous amount of time and effort and transport to get the carpets into a usable condition. Tapestry is very light, too — some people find the carpet bags too heavy for them. So far, despite our success in selling, Carpet Bags has not been as profitable as you might imagine. It's a turn-over business rather than a profit business. The money comes in all right, but most of it goes out again, to the operatives. That's because it's labour-intensive — a lot of people have to do a lot of things just to produce one bag. We're hoping that the Quartey 6-of-6 Range will change that — it's offering 6 proven bag designs each in a choice of 6 tapestries from stock, or hundreds more by special order. We still want to employ as many workers, even more if we can, but it would be good to improve our productivity, and streamline our costs.

When we began we got our carpets from everywhere — from the local market, jumble sales, auctions, friends. We've taken carpets from rubbish tips — and sold them as bags to Harrods. But they will last longer, through our work, than the people who bought them. Now, as well as still getting them from all those sources, we buy them half a ton at a time from 'textile reprocessors' — or scrap dealers! We used to take them into the local launderette to wash them — dirty, smelly, filthy things they were when they first came to us, matted and full of grit, their lovely colours all clouded. The manageress of the launderette was very nice, she didn't seem to mind at all, all that mess and wool clogging up her machines. But then the place closed down (I hope it wasn't our fault!) and we took them to a local laundry. That didn't last long either. So now we have to take them to a commercial laundry, which means travelling *miles.* But they come up beautifully, fresh and brightly coloured again. They are double-washed with pure soap, and then treated with our own special, highly secret techniques to

make them soft and flexible, but strong. Then every bag is cut out by hand and individually made up on a sewing-machine. The first bags were sewn on an ancient bootmaker's treadle-machine. Now we have several heavy industrial machines, old Singers. We've found that they are the only things that will go through four layers of washed carpet, and we picked them up for peanuts in a back street. We also use a marvell-ous Singer overlocker, which is wonderful for doing the straps and all the edgings. We have to use special needles, and very tough, unbreak-able natural threads, to double-stitch the seams and triple-stitch the corners. As far as the actual making is concerned I'm mainly involved in the 'hardware' side, the frames. These are very im-portant, both for appearance *and* usability. We used to buy frames but our sources are closing down, one by one, all over the world. Sadly, nobody is making Gladstone-type frames any longer, so we're having to make a lot of our own, with the help of our blacksmith. They're con-cealed, and almost indestructible.

For the most part there are about a dozen of us involved in Carpet Bags and we can all do just about everything. Some people in the local area do a lot of the cutting and sewing for us — I wouldn't so much call them 'outworkers' as 'in-and-out workers' because their times are very flexible. Sometimes they work in the centre and sometimes they take work home. As well as the making, though, there's all the other side of it, publicity, selling, fetching and carrying, buying fabric, design — all sorts of jobs.

At first *every* stage in the setting up of the business was a matter of overcoming hazards — getting enough carpet, getting the carpet clean, treating it properly, finding machines that would work both effectively and quickly, scouring the world for frames, getting the design prototypes right, finding the *time* — problems, problems. But Loretta and I haven't been making films for the last two years so we've been able to put more and more of our energies into Carpet Bags. Now we're trying to nudge it from a small operation into a big business. That's why we've diversified into tapestry bags, and it's working — thirty a day are going through Liberty's already. In the early days we had no idea of what would sell.

Some of our bags turned out to be what we'd call 'Muldooners' — disasters. But we've gradually learnt what colours and carpet designs are likely to take off, and how to match up the pattern of the carpet with the shape of the bag. For instance, our Slouch Pouch looks good in flowers. The other thing we've discovered is that different shops cater for different tastes — some are flowery, some more sophisticated. We always have a policy of changing absolutely *anything* and if we go to a shop and find that our last delivery is still sitting there we'll take the old stock away and put some different bags on the shelves. Things that aren't popular in the shops we can usually sell from craft fairs and our Green

Desert Tree Fairs.

Our bags travel all over the world — on trains, planes and buses, through cities and across deserts — and are really tested before the designs are offered for sale, and it can take up to two years for us to be sure that they're right. But when we are satisfied, we know that they'll do the job they were designed for, and last and last. Now we see people wearing them and carrying them about all over the place and we still get a charge out of that. The first time it happened we were so excited we nearly crashed the car. It's really good knowing you've made something useful and beautiful out of an otherwise 'waste material', and that somebody is enjoying it.

ANN KINSEY
Machine-knitter

I was always a hand-knitter, ever since I was about 12. My godmother taught me to knit. I remember her standing behind me with her arms around me showing me how to do it. I tried to teach my own daughters the same way but it didn't seem to work with them. For years and years I just knitted for myself and my family. When I was first married — that's twenty-one years ago — I bought a knitting-machine. I didn't go out to work and I just wanted something to occupy myself really. I bought a Singer, and I knitted little tiny garments. I had no children of my own then so I got rid of them on my sister's children and my next-door neighbour's. Money didn't come into it. I didn't think I was experienced enough then to charge people, I was just doing it for the satisfaction. That phase lasted eighteen months and then I went back to my needles again. I preferred my needles really. I put my machine back into the box and put it under the bed. It was lonely, knitting away on my machine in a room at the top of the house, all by myself. So I sold it.

Then, about five years ago, I was browsing round Singers — looking for dress material actually — and there I saw this knitting-machine, staring me in the eyes. It was called a Memomatic. It had punch cards, computerised. I en-

quired about the price and what-have-you, went home and got round my husband, and the long and the short of it was, I had it for my birthday. It was pretty expensive — £300 or £400. When you bought the machine you had a women come and give you a couple of lessons, teaching you the basics, but in fact the basics came back to me from using the old machine. It wasn't difficult, but the punch cards I had to learn because I didn't have them on my other one.

I was still knitting just for the family but you can't keep on knitting jumpers and jumpers. Our wardrobes are stuffed full anyway. But then I knitted a jumper that didn't fit anybody in the family so I took it along to my mother and her neighbour took it along to the dancing school where her daughters went — and somebody bought it. That was the beginning. I did have lots of wool. I'm really one for wool. Even if I don't need it I have to have it. Next thing, my daughter said she wanted a sweater. 'All different colours, all stripes, all the colours you've got here,' she said. But when it was finished it didn't fit her, so again it went off to the dancing school and all the children wanted one. I was really sick of doing them. I must have made a couple of dozen, easy. And then my daughter said if everybody else was wearing them she didn't want one. She'd thought it would be something different! I only charged from £3 to £5 for them. I went by what the prices were in the shops and charged less. People aren't keen to pay a lot, you know. I was never dear, that's why I got so many orders. It took a long time, a lot of work, doing the stripes, changing the colours, sewing in the long threads left at the ends, but I never worked out my hours. I just charged what I thought people would pay. I wasn't earning a bomb. I was just glad to knit something for somebody. We have so many sweaters in this house it's a family joke. My husband will say, 'This jumper's dirty, can you knit me a new one?' After the stripey jumpers the next craze at the dancing school was sweaters with a sports motif. The girls were very keen on those. Then I knitted a lot of school uniform jumpers. But all that died a natural death because my friend's daughters gave up dancing, so I lost that contact.

A year ago I was introduced to a local knitting club and I go there once a month. They have people come and give you ideas, show you what they knit, what yarns they use, what machines they work on. It's just a place to swop ideas really. Designers come and talk to us, and people with shops.

I've got rid of my Memomatic now, and I have a Knitmaster 360. It was recommended to me by different people. And it has a lace carriage that I was interested in, and you can buy different attachments for it — a weavemaster, a yarn changer, a rib transfer carriage, that sort of thing. People go on asking me to make them things, funny things sometimes. There was a Roman Catholic priest who wanted a grey cardigan with pockets, and he had a 48-inch chest. Two challenges — I'd never knitted a pocket before, and I'd never made such a large garment. It only just sat on my machine. I'm into lacy things now. Lace cardigans. I'm sick to death of the things. I made one for my mother but it was too short in the body so I took it along to one of my knitting friends. She can't get out very much and always has lots of people visiting her, seeing what she's got on the go. One of her visitors took the lace cardigan to work, sold it, and came back with an order for six more. Now I've done another dozen, and the phone's still ringing, asking for more. But you do get bored, doing exactly the same pattern all the time. The

other big thing is matinée jackets. I've just done six, but with them, every one is different. I can make three matinée jackets in a day, fitting it in between shopping and housework and picking up my children from school. I'm selling the jackets through a party-plan organiser. She took one of them to a party and there was such a lot of interest she's asked me to do lots more. She's also ordered slash-necked, tuck-stitch sweaters, as many as I can do. I don't want to be pressured, though. I like just going on steadily, not having to hurry to get things done by a certain date. Just keeping busy.

My family is the important thing and my girls — I have two, one is 16, the other 8 — want to talk to me and have me around during the evening. And they don't want the noise and clatter of a knitting-machine going. So I stop knitting at 5 o'clock and then at 8 I'll start sewing up garments. That keeps me awake, but I'm not making a noise and interfering with the family. I have a special room for the knitting-machine. I used to be shoved off in the spare bedroom but I didn't like that. I like to be around with the family, so now I share a room with my husband. He's a bee-keeper and he needs a space for his books and equipment, where he can do artificial insemination, so we have one room between us. The trouble is, my wool keeps spreading into his half. It gets all over the place. I don't buy it wholesale. I get it from the shop where I bought my machine. I prefer not to buy too large a quantity at a time because I don't want to be lumbered with wool I may not use. I buy three magazines from the shop, too. The most useful I've found are *Knitting Digest* which comes out about every two months, and *Modern Knitting* which is another two-monthly publication. The other is *World of Knitting* which comes out monthly. I can hardly wait for them — they're filled with patterns, and ideas, and new techniques, and *Modern Knitting* is *really* modern, knitted suits and what-have-you.

I've made all sorts of things in my time — sweaters, shawls, leg-warmers, mittens, scarves, suits for myself, a dress for my daughter. I enjoy the baby clothes most, the shawls and matinée jackets, because I love babies, I suppose. I'm just sorry that when mine were born I'd gone off knitting altogether, put my machine away *and* gone off the needles. I spend the money I earn on my kids. And I also buy more wool, of course, and new parts for the machine. They're not cheap. I'm saving up now to buy an electronic knitting-machine. I knit purely for satisfaction and something to do. I'd be lost without it, I really would, but it is just a paying hobby because the family comes first. Even when the girls leave home I'll still have my husband to look after, and I help him with his bee-keeping so I can't see myself doing much

more. I have no plans to change or develop.

In a way I'd like to have a wool shop, I really would. There's a little shop close by that my friend and I say we'd like to take over if ever it came on the market, have a knitting-machine in the window, and do knitting to order as well as selling wool. But my husband's in business and I know only too well what the bills can be like, and the worries. So I'm quite happy the way things are, having it as an interest, making a bit of money. It's the satisfaction that matters, and having people *wear* the things I knit.

RUSTY GRIMMOND
Soft-toymaker
'Rustoys'

I first started making money out of soft toys purely by chance about ten years ago. Dogs are my great passion. I show them and breed them. I saw a pattern in a magazine for a great big soft-toy dog to lie against a door and use as a

Handmade
in
Norfolk
by
RUSTOYS

draught-excluder. He was really lovely and I thought, 'I'll make one of those and put him under the television set. He'll look nice there.' Well, I went out, bought the material, made him up, and my daughter said could she take him to work to show her friends. Then she rang me up from work and said would I like to sell him. I said I hadn't thought of that, I'd made him for myself, and she said couldn't I sell that one to her friend and make another one for myself. By the time she came home she had orders for twenty-six and in the end I sold three hundred altogether — all in fur fabric, every colour imaginable.

I really *enjoy* making soft toys. I always loved making things at school — kettle-holders out of scraps of felt, that sort of thing. That was always my favourite lesson. So when I saw that Norwich City Council Amenities was advertising for stall-holders for Blackfriars Craft Fair, which is held in the cloisters of St Andrew's in Norwich on Satur-

days, I rang up and found out more about it and I thought, 'I'd like to do that.' At first there was such a big response to the advertisement that I could only have a stall when someone else cancelled, but soon I got a regular stall of my own. I pay £8 a day for it. It suits me very well. I love it, meeting all the people, and the other craftsmen. Summer is rather slack. A lot of the stall-holders and the customers are out at country fairs and agricultural shows all over the place so there's not so much business in Norwich itself, but Christmas time is very busy. I sell so much for Christmas presents that on Christmas Day I really feel quite nervous, thinking about all those people opening their parcels and getting something I've made, and I'm just *hoping* that they like them. I can't really believe that my toys are good enough to give that much pleasure, but people seem to be well satisfied. Most of them go to adults rather than children. Men buy them for their wives. They'll come up to me on the stall when their wives are with them and whisper, 'You will be here next week, won't you?', and then they'll come back on their own to buy something that's caught her eye.

Plate 5   Cushions, from top to bottom: lace cushion and lace flowers from Jane Playford, Jane's Pincushion; two satin ribbon-weave cushions from Marilyn Becker, Ribbon Designs; scented butterfly and rose patchwork cushions from Libby Calvert; satin ice cream cone and racing car cushions from Janet Grant, Moonraker Designs; patchwork cushions from Anna Potten

About two years ago a new craft centre was opening nearby, and the organiser of Blackfriars was asked if he could recommend a toymaker who would provide good soft toys for the centre's gallery shop. He put my name forward and I was asked to go along and have a chat and show him what I made. I liked the place but I was amazed when they said they just wanted to sell things for under £2, and that was the price *after* they'd put their commission on. I agreed to do it, because I can make little owls and chickens and mice for less than that, but I knew that they would be able to sell my big things, even at £25 each. My speciality is really *big* toys, so large that they can be used as children's pouffes, floor cushions or foot-stools. I do a lovely sleepy-eyed hippo, a fat, black silky pig that measures about a foot and a half by two and a half feet, a great big pink elephant, a stripey tiger, huge lions and dogs, afghans and chows, and snake draught-excluders that are a good three feet long. Well, they agreed to take some of the big things as well as the little ones, puppets and tiny teddies, and they were absolutely staggered at how well they went. They've gone on being a splendid outlet for me because thousands of people visit the crafts centre all through the year and there's a very fast turn-over. They only work on a sale-or-return basis, and I know that a lot of craftspeople say that's not a very good idea, but I like it with them because they let me get on with it. I can go in at any time, arrange my own display so that the toys are shown off to their best advantage, take in what I like, change anything that's not selling, write my own cards. I feel part of the enterprise — it's almost like having my own shop.

My goods need constant attention, you see, regular grooming and brushing up, or they get untidy. One day when I went in some child had pushed a bit of sticky rock up my hippo's nose. I poked it out but it needed wiping clean so I marched the hippo off to the toilet to wash his face. There was a poor man sitting outside mind-ing his own business. He watched me carry the hippo into the ladies' loo, then carry him out again saying, 'There, you feel better for that, don't you?' You should have seen his face. He obviously thought I'd gone quite mad. 'Loony lady takes toy hippo to ladies' loo!'

I make a lovely standing grizzly bear with his paw stretched out. Just like Max Bygraves — 'I wanna tell you a story.' I used to stuff him well so that he was really firm and upright, and I thought people might hang their umbrellas over his arm and use him as a hat-stand — I like my toys to be *used* — but he didn't sell for ages. One day I went along to the centre to take a look at him and I thought — too much stuffing, that's the trouble. So I got him down on the floor there and then, cut him open, pulled out masses and masses of stuffing — washable acrylic fibre I use. It was all over the place, customers looking at me in amazement, picking their way through the stuff. When I sewed him up he looked much softer, so I laid him on his back and wrote a new card saying: 'Floor cushion — you may sit on my tummy if you like.' He sold straight away! Then I made another big bear for a car cushion — sensational lolling on the back window ledge. He sold, too.

The stuffing is vital. It must be well done if the toy is going to look good. You have to get it right down to the extremities, properly packed in, and the right amount, not too much, not too little. The difficulty is, the material stretches if you push too hard so you have to be careful not to let it get out of shape. I stuff my toys myself and add all the finishing details, but I have two helpers who I pay for piece-work. One of them can machine the big things for me, the other concentrates on the smaller ones and she can machine them and cut them out. We work to a hundred patterns altogether. I've had such a lot of work recently that I'm expanding and advertising for a third helper, through a card in a local shop window. It'll be interesting to see who I'll get, what sort of skills she will have to offer.

I used to work in the sitting-room — fluff everywhere, an awful mess! — but now that my daughters have married and left home I've taken over their rooms. I'm gradually taking over the whole house — my husband will be next to go! I use a heavy old Pfaff domestic sewing-machine,

Plate 6   Silk batik kite from Anna Potten; hand dyed and batik silk kimono, and quilted silk shoes, from Lene Bragger, Hillside Crafts; silk scarves from Pat Johnston, Handmade

very basic but I love it. My husband wants me to have a super new one but I say no, this will do me fine until it falls to bits. I'm *used* to it. We put the two bedside units against a wall and laid a length of conti-board across them and hey presto! there was my work bench with storage drawers underneath. I buy eyes and noses by the hundred, and those I keep in those little plastic drawers that do-it-yourself men use for nails and screws. Each drawer is labelled 'pink triangular noses', 'character eyes with lashes', 'woggle eyes', or whatever, so that I can find what I need at a glance. I have yards and yards of fur fabric, all colours and textures, hanging in the wardrobes and spread out in layers on the beds, waiting to be used. I was recommended to go to Oakley Fabrics in Luton for fabric, and though I have tried other firms I'm very pleased with them. Their prices are really competitive, and they supply stuffing, noses and eyes as well as material. I always get £100 worth of goods at a time because if you do that you can get half-price bargain packs as a bonus, smaller pieces that can be made up in all sorts of ways. In the last pack there was some white fur fabric with the pile lying the wrong way so it was a second, but I wondered what to do with it and suddenly saw that it would be perfect for the fluffy breast of a baby owl, just like feathers. I sometimes go to my local supplier, too — Anglian Fashion Fabrics — because I think it's a good thing to support firms in your own area if you can. I get pretty little cream and brown swing-tickets from a printer at the crafts centre. Printed with 'Handmade in Norfolk by Rustoys', one is sewn on to every item.

I keep trying out new things — that's important, or you get stale. I'm doing a lovely frog puppet now, a big one that you put your arm through and manipulate the mouth with your hand. My *grown-up* son plays about with him for hours — he's a bit like Kermit, vivid green with a bright red gaping mouth and a very expressive face. And for something different I've made a cot quilt or wall-hanging, appliquéd with a teddy, and nightdress cases the same, all in lovely soft fur fabric, of course.

I find patterns to give me ideas and then adapt them to my own design. I get soft-toymaking books from the library, but just to look at and think about, not to work from. My really invaluable reference books are my encyclopaedia of dogs, and my nature books of animals, so that I can study photographs and detailed drawings and get them absolutely right. When I did my badger I realised I didn't know *exactly* what a badger looked like, so I had to look one up and study its shape and colouring.

Actually, I started working at selling toys to pay the costs of showing my dogs. That's an expensive hobby. My husband would have been happy to pay but I felt better making my own contribution. Now I make more than I need for that but there's no doubt at all, it's a labour of love. I wouldn't like to live off what I make. I just charge about £2 an hour for my labour — sometimes I up it, and sometimes bring it down, depending on the market value of what I've made. People will pay a lot for the big things, you see, but it's the little fiddly ones that really take the *time;* much less material but hours of labour. Blackfriars Craft Fair and the Craft Centre Gallery are my only outlets, apart from private orders. I'm not so keen on those because I do worry a bit when people ask me to make them something special, wonder whether I've got it quite right, whether they'll be really pleased with it. It's much easier if they just see something that's finished and buy that — then you know that it's exactly what they want. I could find more outlets easily enough, I suppose, and make much more money if I worked really hard at it, but I don't want to. There are other things I like doing. I'm a wife and mother, and I have my dogs and my garden — my latest passion is growing fuchsias. Besides, the only way you can produce things in great quantities is to employ a lot of outworkers, and I don't want that. I think the reason my toys are popular is because I like them and care about them and give them the personal touch. They're all individuals. A little while ago a lady asked me to do her a pekinese because her pet had just died. She gave me a photograph and I studied it in my dogs' encyclopaedia and made her what she wanted. And she was so thrilled! It was almost as if she had her pet back again. I was really pleased that she was so happy, and you couldn't get *that* sort of satisfaction if it was a proper, high-powered business.

SELMA HARRIS
Needlewoman/Designer

I trained in fashion design and took a degree at Bournemouth College of Art, and to start with I worked for a London company that made theatrical costumes. But I soon decided that fashion design wasn't for me. It wasn't the clothes I made that interested me, but what I did to them, the decoration, appliqué, beadwork, that sort of thing. So I moved on to interior design.

I still make clothes, but only wedding dresses, to order. That appeals to me — it's something very very nice, something special. I made my own, of course, and then my sister's, and one for a friend, and then people started asking me to make *their* dresses for them. When I made one about a year ago the bride and I worked out the dress together. We had in mind Thai silk and Victorian lace to make it in. I designed it, but before I made it up I thought we should go to Harrods to see if they had anything similar so that she could see what she would look like when it was finished. She tried one on and it cost £850, and the sales lady said the same dress could be made up to any customer's specific size. We bought the material for hers, better quality than Harrods, the fabric, lining and interlining all of pure silk, and trimmed with lace, and it only cost us £120. So someone, somewhere along the line, was making a lot of profit — six girls might have walked into the store and ordered that wedding dress in one week.

For me, wedding dresses are only a side-line. When I stopped working in fashion design I set up as an interior design consultant. I would design people's flats for them, the whole thing, colours, furnishings, fabrics, decorations, and then get sub-contractors to do the work to my specification. That wasn't a success really because of the hassles about money. Some of my customers just wouldn't pay my contractors the right price for the full amount of work they'd done, or they were late in paying, and *I* felt responsible. I was the middle man. I know now that I was doing things the wrong way. I should have put a clause in the contract saying that payment to the contractors was the responsibility of the customer, not mine. But I didn't know that. If I'd known *then* what I know now it would have been a very different story, but it's too late now because I'm so happy with my present work that I wouldn't go back to that. Now I do a job where the customer gives me an order, takes my work, pays the money, then says 'Goodbye'. That's nice. In interior design it never *ends.*

What I do now is design and make home furnishings — window-blinds, bedcovers, lamp-shades, cushions, decorative wall panels and mobiles. In the beginning I made things I wanted but couldn't find in the shops, so I knew other people wouldn't be able to buy them anywhere else except through me. I did a lot of original things, especially for children's rooms. I think I like designing for baby bedrooms most of all because that's something different. I do quilted, padded cot covers with special appliqués — one of the covers is appliquéd with a picture of a fairy castle rising up out of the clouds. Padded appliqué pictures on boards, sort of fabric murals, are a speciality, and three-dimensional shapes that hang from the ceiling.

I do clouds, shaped to spell out a child's name — LEE would have a big fat capital 'L' joined up to two cloud-shaped 'E's, with suspended crystal rain-drops sewn on to them. I've made lots of those — children love them, something special with their name spelt on it. The other favourite is an icecream mobile, a '99' cone, with little droplets of icecream hanging off and a big brown woolly chocolate flake. Both the fairy castle and the icecream cone designs are available on window-blinds, too, either painted or appliquéd, very bright and colourful. Three flavours of icecream *and* a lovely red cherry!

At present my special lines for adult décor are window-blinds painted with English flowers, and accessories to match, especially satin cushions. For a special commission I made a quilted bedcover from 9-inch squares of satin silk, every alternate square decorated with a different flower, foxgloves, hollyhocks, sweetpeas . . . I don't do as much appliqué work now as I used to because it takes such a long time that if you charge for your labour by the hour you can't

possibly get a realistic price. Plus the fact that John Lewis's started importing beautiful appliquéd goods from Taiwan and Hong Kong which they could sell at less than the actual materials would have cost me, and they were lovely. My things would have had to cost about three times as much, and I wouldn't have paid the extra if I'd been a customer. You do have to watch the shops, and the current fashions, and change your product accordingly. Tastes keep changing, and so does availability. And people lose interest if the shops are flooded with the same sort of goods — they want something different.

I sell in two different ways, either to individuals on direct commission, or by special order through interior design shops. I don't really like selling to friends because of the difficulty of charging. If you want to make money you have to force yourself to be impersonal, treat every transaction as a business deal. If you sell privately and people know that you're working from home and you're a 'mum' they seem to think they should have things at jumble sale prices and get quite upset if you charge properly. I have a scale of charges — the basic cost of materials plus a fee of £15 an hour if I sell privately, £7.50 an hour if I sell through shops, because I know they have to put on their overheads and I don't want to price myself out of the market. You have to make a choice — either you're selling privately and making a bigger profit on each item but selling less of them, or you can sell commercially for a smaller profit but in larger quantities. I combine both. To find my commercial outlets first of all I chose local shops that looked good, had the same sort of tastes as mine and seemed to attract a lot of customers, then I took samples of blinds, bedcovers, lampshades and cushions to show them. Then I went up to London, to Chelsea and Knightsbridge. Everywhere I went they wanted at least one blind to put on display along with a notice to say they would take orders to special requirements, and one shop is filling a whole window with a full range of the things I make. My goods are so individual and specialised that they only appeal to a certain type of customer so this way of selling to order is the best way of marketing them. In this way a customer can decide on her own choice of colours, what sort of flowers she wants, whether she'd like matching cushions, bedspread, lampshades, everything.

In the world of the interior design, shops' charges bear no relation to reality. They can go sky high. It's a luxury market and customers believe that if they're paying a lot for something it must be good. I've seen bedspreads costing £1,600 — I couldn't believe it! These people don't think twice about spending £20 or £30 on a cushion, but if they saw exactly the same thing in a craft market priced at £3 they wouldn't think it was worth it. At that price it must be rubbish! Buyers don't bat an eyelid when I say I charge £15 an hour for private work, so I think it makes sense to 'go for broke'.

This all makes me sound very hard-headed and business-like, even cynical, but it wasn't always the case. When I began I did the soft furnishings for a whole room — curtains, blinds, bedspread, all very decorative and luxurious, trimmed with lace, and curtains stretched on a pole behind the head of the bed, scatter cushions piled on the bed, even elegant tie-backs. *And* I covered a piano stool to transform it into a dressing-table stool. I'd never done that before so I had to teach myself. It took me days and *days,* and for all that I only charged £120. That was when I was in the transition stage between hobby and business. But then something happened that completely changed my attitude. My husband was made redundant. I suddenly thought, 'What have I been *doing*? I've been trained, I have a degree, yet I've never really earned my own living, just a bit extra. I haven't taken my work seriously. I only have one child and I'm not planning to have another. There's no reason at all why I shouldn't make my hobby into a proper business, learn to support myself.' I'm very fortunate in having a friendly neighbour who happens to be a bank manager. He was marvellous. He was on holiday and he spent a whole week helping me to work out how to make my time cost-effective, checking on everything I was doing, pointing out where I was going wrong, showing me how I could improve. He told me that craftspeople are notorious with bankers for being unbusiness-like. Hundreds of them go under because they won't cost their time and won't change their product to suit the demands of the market. They start off working from home, buying their materials at retail prices, not charging for their hours, and hardly even covering their costs initially. That's fine if you're doing it for fun — but if it was just fun I was after I'd rather be spending more time with my son and my friends, helping my husband who is now self-employed and working from home. But if it's an income you're after you have to be business-like. You have to work out how much you think you should earn for a day's work, what your skill and training is worth. Then you should divide that sum by eight and fix an hourly charge. Next you have to think about how much time goes into what you're making, and whether the price you have to charge for it is reasonable. If it's not — make something else. The ideal is something that is relatively quick and easy to make but looks both good and complicated. For example, I've made beautiful, stylish sequinned cushions with a structured design. They take me hours to do, and if a shop bought them and paid me for my time and then put their 100 per cent on top of that they would be impossible to sell. The price would be ludicrous. In the same time it takes me to do one sequinned cushion I can do a dozen hand-painted cushions — so, I've dropped the sequins and gone for the hand-painting. I used to make all my own blinds — until I discovered that I could buy them wholesale, through a friend who has a curtain business, for the same price as it cost me to make them, and just as good. So now I buy the blinds and decorate them by hand with either paint or appliqué, whichever the customer prefers. I have a big portfolio of designs that they can choose from.

I didn't have any capital to draw on when I began, and I couldn't tap my husband's resources because he was setting up in business on his own account, but I did need money to buy materials. I got out of this by calculating the number of hours' work that would be involved in any commission I was offered, adding in the cost of materials and arriving at an estimated price. Then I asked for a third of that in advance, a third halfway through, and the rest of the *actual* price

— it might be a little more or a little less than the original estimate, depending on how I'd got on — on delivery.

I work out my day on an organised basis if possible. After I've taken my son to school the first thing I do is deal with my correspondence, checking any orders that have come in and dealing with any bills that have to be paid. Then I either go out selling, seeing interior design buyers, showing them my work and getting orders, or I stay at home and work on the orders I've already got. Now I've reached the stage where I could earn my own living if I worked flat out, 9 to 5, five days a week. But as it is I do a four-day week because I have my son to look after, and I do my husband's books for him. It's a nice feeling, knowing that, with luck, I'll never have to worry again at the thought of not being able to pay my own way if necessary.

JANET GRANT
Satin Cushion-maker
'Moonraker Designs'

I worked in London for a short time as a graphic designer — I had trained at Salisbury College of Art — and I used to go along to John Lewis's in Oxford Street and buy remnants of satin. They had loads of it and I really liked the fabric. The colours are so marvellous, and the texture. I used to buy the material just because I loved it, I didn't know what I would do with it. Then one day when I was wondering how I would use it a friend of mine — he's an artist — suggested I make him a cushion in the shape of a tube of paint. The idea really appealed to me. It was something different, and I really enjoyed making it. I put a blob of paint on the end of the tube and the idea worked really well.

That was in October three years ago. By that time I'd come back to Salisbury from London and did knitting. I had a knitting-machine and sold sweaters and things at craft fairs. My husband Alex and I work together. He makes glass terrariums and we share a stall at the fairs we go to. I wasn't particularly happy about the sweaters. People always wanted different sizes and colours. 'Haven't you got a size 16?', they'd say. And there were lots of other people knitting, so I was looking around for something different to do when my friend came up with the idea of the cushion. We'd done two Christmas craft fairs with the terrariums and my knitting at Salisbury Arts Centre, and we'd booked our stall again, so I decided to do cushions that year instead.

I don't know how I'd describe them. I suppose they should be called novelty cushions but I don't like the name. But they're not really practical. They're just for fun. Fun cushions, you could call them. They can be washed, though. I've never washed one but one of my customers told me she had. 'Put it in the spin-drier and it came up lovely,' she said. They're stuffed with washable polyester filling so they should be all right.

The first year I did pencil cushions — they were popular and still are — and icecream cones, all in lots of bright colours. The icecream cones are the things that people notice most, and talk about. And I did rainbows, and stars and moons. There wasn't an awful lot of designs, or stock, but it went very well and I sold everything, including the tube of paint, so my friend still hasn't had it. I put it on the stall to make it look as if I had lots of things to sell and it just went. I keep telling him I'll make another when I have time.

Now I've branched out into new designs. I make pairs of cushions that go together in one polythene pack. As well as the moon-and-star there's thunder-and-lightning, and cloud-and-sun. I sometimes do racing cars in very bright shiny colours. They're very fiddly to make and I love them but I have to charge quite a lot for them and they don't go as well as some of the other things. I've just started doing flowers — they're quite new — but I'm not sure yet whether they're a success. Sometimes I do a one-off design, like a paint-brush or a cigar. And I make icecream cones and ice-lollies as brooches which I can sell for under £1 so people can just

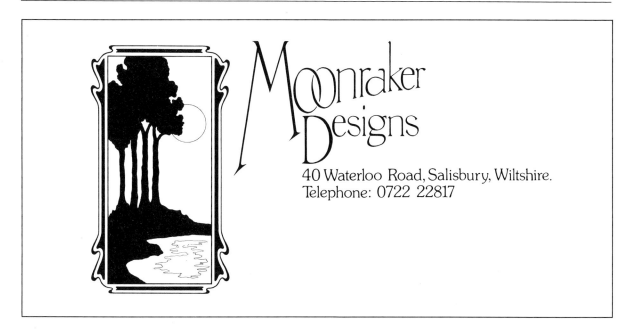

Moonraker Designs

40 Waterloo Road, Salisbury, Wiltshire.
Telephone: 0722 22817

buy them out of the money in their purses without having to think too hard about it. I do sometimes feel they're awfully unwilling to pay a fair price for something that's taken me hours and hours of work. The pencil cushions are cheap — less than £5 — and they go just like that, but I have to charge more for the racing cars so they go slowly, which doesn't sound right for a racing car! The thing I really like is my ham sandwich. A friend got a new brief-case and of course every brief-case needs a ham sandwich so I made him a lovely one with a thick slice of ham and bits of tomato and lettuce squeezing out round the edges of the slices of bread. That went down so well I've made a few more.

One of the nice things about making the cushions is that they complement Alex's terrariums. Satin looks much better with glass than wool does. The stall looks really lovely and there's always a crowd round it. We set our things out on Indian bedspreads. To start with we used them just because we had them, but then people said how distinctive they looked and how well they went with the terrariums, so we stuck with them. The trouble with the cushions is that people always want to pick them up and fiddle about with them, feel them, and pull at the edges. They'll pick up an icecream cone and pre-

tend to lick it. They're just being funny really, but I stand there trying to smile and thinking, 'Oh, I've made them so carefully and they're just messing about with them.'

We only sell through craft fairs. We have tried shops but people just like to buy one or two to start with and really they need a big display to look good. We do eight to ten fairs a year, and things like steam rallies in the summer. We don't go far from Salisbury — last weekend we were at Winchester and Wilton House. We went to Abingdon last Christmas but no further afield than Oxfordshire really. We try to get around as much as we can at Christmas because that's when we sell most of our stuff. There are so *many* craft fairs these days. People see our work in one place and then invite us to go to others — because our stuff is so different, I suppose, and there's nothing else quite like it. They send us details and ask if we'd like to take a stall. The trick is to decide which will be a good place to go to. You can't always tell from just reading the information they send.

Apart from our goods and bedspreads all we need really when we go to a fair is transport. We didn't have a car or anything when we began so we bought a dinky little red van. It's got a small engine and it's quite good on petrol so really it's ideal for what we need, and we both drive it.

We have one big room set aside in our house where we work. I use a big table with an ordinary domestic sewing-machine and an overlocker — that's for doing the inside edges to prevent them from fraying. And I have my iron and ironing-board there. And lots and lots of shelves for storage, that's for packaging as well as materials. Every item I make goes into its own polythene bag and then the cushions get stacked away in big black plastic sacks — a sackful of rainbows, and a sackful of flowers, and so on. I still buy my satin from John Lewis's because I do need to rely on getting exactly the same quality and the same colours again.

I'm afraid I fix my prices by guess! Alex is very particular about his costing. He charges an hourly rate for his time and writes down all his expenses and then adds them all together. But I don't do it like that. I've just got an idea now of what people will pay. I don't really allow anything for my hours. I suppose I work roughly to twice the cost of my materials. Cushions that I do a lot of I can make in batches of twelve and that makes the work much quicker. More unusual things, that I make two at a time, take much longer. But that's the nice thing of not actually having to make a living out of it. At present I have a part-time job and Alex works full-time. If the craft work were our sole means of income we'd have to be much stricter with our pricing and look for more selling outlets. We don't work as hard as you might imagine. We try to keep things going steadily but when there are craft fairs coming up, especially at Christmas, we work harder, then afterwards we flop and that's it for a while. As a general rule we never work past nine at night. Then we stop, have supper, watch television perhaps. We keep reminding ourselves that the whole point, at the beginning, was to do this for our own satisfaction, so we're not knocking ourselves out working through the night or any-thing like that.

We do run it as a proper business, though. All the money we make goes straight back into the funds and then we buy more materials. Since we don't trade under our own names we had to register our business when we started, but that's all changed now. We have an accountant to help us. We keep the books ourselves then once a year he goes over them, fills in the tax returns and deals with the Inland Revenue. It's well worth it really. It was very hard to find a name. We agonised over it for ages and eventually came up with Moonraker Designs, which *we* thought very original. It's from the Wiltshire legend of the smugglers pretending they were raking the water for a cheese when it was really the reflection of the moon. Then, when we found it, we discovered that the name 'Moonraker' is used all over the place. But we're stuck with it now because people seem to remember it. We've never advertised but we've designed our own cards and leaflets and have our own moon-raker logo of the moon in the pond, and we always put those on our stall wherever we go.

We've really been very lucky. When we began we didn't think we would be so popular for so long. The things we are making are fairly frivol-ous and expensive and we thought they'd reach a peak and then go out of fashion, but that hasn't happened yet, thank goodness. On the other hand, we've been doing the same thing for a few years and are now thinking we should do some-thing different, expand, change. We are aiming to make this our main source of income eventu-ally but it's a big step to take, giving up your job. What we'd really like is a place in the country — that's what everyone would like, isn't it? — from which we could sell our things, and other people's, too. And perhaps have craft weekends as well, to teach other people to make things. That would be lovely. But it's a long way ahead, still just a dream.

MARGARET GRANGER
Creative Embroiderer

At present I make small, painted, hand-embroidered pictures — very small, 5 inches square, 7 inches square when they're framed — and large patchwork wall-hangings. Machine-made cushions and quilts, too, but not so often. I started off in this direction after a City and Guilds Embroidery course. It was one day a week officially, but there was masses of homework to do so it felt almost full-time, and it lasted for two years. It was mostly about design — lots of design, colour appreciation, visiting museums and galleries to study embroideries, then actually *doing* embroidery at home. It's a very stimulating course. I'd recommend it to anyone that way inclined. It's jolly hard work, though. I did it when my last child started school because then I thought that time was going to be hanging heavily on my hands, but gosh! there was no chance of that!

My first job, before I was married, was in dental nursing, but I'd always been interested in needlework as a hobby so it was lovely to be able to go into it properly and then make it a sort of second career. When the City and Guilds course ended I got together with a friend who had been on it with me and we decided to work together. We each invested £50 and bought lots of different materials to get started. That would be in October '77 so the prices I'm quoting will have gone up a bit since then. It's a good idea starting with a partner — it gives you that initial confidence you need when it comes to the stage of taking things to the shops. To begin with we made cushions — a dozen patchwork cushions — and we piled them into the back of my Mini and went off to Dorking. There was a designer-type shop there that sold lots of nice things, stripped pine furniture and pottery, and so on, and we'd decided that our cushions would complement the rest of the goods. You do need to look for the right *sort* of shop. We marched in and the owner said yes, he'd be very interested, but he gave us a terribly low price for them. We agreed to it, but we were very disappointed. Then he ordered another dozen, still at the same low price, and we were just beginners so we made those for him, too — but after that we called it a day as far as he was concerned. We wanted to be paid the cost of the materials plus £2 an hour for our labour. Actually the materials cost us £4 and he paid us £5 for each cushion. Only £1 for labour and they really took quite a long time to make. There was a lot of careful work in them. He sold them for £10.99 each, and *then* we saw a photograph of them in *Ideal Home* magazine, advertising his shop. We were very annoyed — we felt he had used us badly.

After that experience we decided it would be a good idea to have stalls at craft markets, and this was much better. We made our stall look good, covering boxes with neutral-coloured hessian to set off the colours of the cushions, making an attractive display at various heights. We charged £7.50 for a cushion — we thought this was a reasonable price because they were made from Liberty's material, expensive, very good quality. We still went on selling to shops, though, and found several outlets that were more realistic financially, as well as getting lots of orders from friends. We did quite well, in fact, and were able to buy ourselves new sewing-machines. We only advertised once, in a glossy magazine, and we got *one* query, that's all. Someone wrote and asked us to send photographs of what we made. We weren't given an order, and the photographs weren't returned — so that was another disaster story.

Meanwhile, we were making our first patchwork quilt, the two of us making it together. It turned out to be gorgeous, though I shouldn't really say it; but it was absolutely lovely. It was bought by a lady from Australia who wanted it for her king-size brass bedstead, so it went out there. We didn't let it go straight away. At first we

---

Margaret Granger

Embroidery & Watercolour Paintings

Ashtead 75486

---

kept it, to show what we could do. We hung it up at the back of the stall at craft fairs; people saw it and ordered one for themselves on the strength of that, and we sold ten altogether.

Family Circle did a feature about the quilts and cushions. We saw that they were doing a series on crafts people so we contacted them, telephoned. They said they would like to write us up and sent a journalist down to interview us.

In fact, what we really wanted to do was embroidery. That was what we'd wanted to do initially but we'd somehow got side-tracked into the patchwork and quilting. We began to make the embroidered pictures to sell along with the patchwork. We thought they'd go well together. They just came out of our heads. We'd evolved this idea of working on calico with paint *and* embroidery. We spent one day a week working together, and in the summer when the weather was good we'd go out and sketch locally, just landscapes that appealed to us, and built up a collection of sketches to work on later. When we brought them home they often had to be altered a bit, to get them properly balanced, turned into a pleasing shape — a tree might have to be made smaller, or a hedge moved to a different angle. Then we painted the picture we'd created on to calico. We did a lot of country views. And sheep. Sheep were the favourites, but I'm also lit up by gardens. Gardens like Wisley, clumps of flowers, leaves . . . the textures you get, and shapes, the patterns they form, and all the wonderful colour. I absolutely love colour. After the calico had been painted we let it dry, ironed it, and then put in all the details of the picture with embroidery silks so that all that was left pure paint was the sky and green fields. You begin to see the countryside in terms of chain-stitch and French knots. A ploughed field would be rows of chain-stitch, different shades of brown, with a few variations for texture. I think, with our particular combination of calico, paint and embroidery we hit on something that hadn't been done before. We didn't need much equipment. The calico has to be embroidered in a frame, that's important, but apart from that — scissors, needles . . . that's all really. The trouble is that silks are expensive to buy and you have to have lots of colours. A tree isn't just green, it's masses of different greens, and to make it look alive you have to use dozens of shades. (We buy embroidery threads from Liberty's, or from the Danish Shop in Sloane Street, or wherever we see a new colour. The calico is bought locally, or from John Lewis's, where they have a wonderful range of materials.) When the pictures were finished we signed them in embroidery thread, tucking the signature away in a clump of flowers, or under a hedge. Then they were ready to be mounted and framed, having been stretched on to a backing of stiff card. We found someone to make the frames and cut the mounts for us. We could do them ourselves because that was one of the things we were taught on our course, but it's not really worth it. They have to be meticulous. The whole presentation must be spotless and beautiful. So, we buy a lot at a time and get them done at a special price. Finally, for the back of the frame, we have Able Label stickers, black on gold, saying who each picture is designed and made by. People like to know, and can always order more if they know how to make contact.

When we had the first dozen pictures together we decided to try to sell them to a shop called Craft Work which was part of Cranks. It sold beautiful things, all made from natural materials, hand-dyed from natural sources. Sadly, because our threads were artificially dyed the buyer couldn't take them but he loved them and suggested we try Liberty's, and another shop that might be right, in Brighton. We wrote to Liberty's and they wrote back and said they were interested and sent us a form to fill in, with all sorts of details such as where we'd done our training, that sort of thing, and then we were invited to take the pictures in to show them. They ordered some straight away, and they've gone on reordering, ten or twelve at a time. The Brighton shop took some, too, but on a sale-or-return basis, so we stopped selling there. Sale-or-return isn't fair on the craftsman. I'd thoroughly discourage anyone from agreeing to that. You have to wait a long time for your money, and then you might just get the goods back again, when you could have sold them somewhere else. And if they're returned they might be shop-soiled and there's nothing you can do about that. It's not a satisfactory system because craftspeople are usually waiting for their money so that they can buy more materials. Other places we sell to are the General Trading Company in Sloane Street which gives us an order for about eight or ten pictures, four times a year, and a shop in Totnes. That was quite interesting — we were selling from a market stall in Reigate when a lady came up looking for stock for a new business she was about to open. She bought nearly everything we had and keeps coming back for more.

Most of these places would take more but the trouble is, each one takes a long time to produce. I've recently lost my partner so I can't make very many on my own. Apart from the sketching of it, and the thinking of it, the actual *sewing* of it takes me about ten hours, I suppose. Sometimes longer, sometimes less, depending on how much detail is in it. Each one is different, unique. I'd be quicker if I made lots the same, but I don't want to do that. Half the fun is making them all originals, trying new things. I've got enough work to keep me busy all the year without being pressured — except at Christmas. Then I'm pressured because everyone wants something and there are all the other demands on my time anyway, the ordinary family things. But it's good to have a little bit of pressure — I think everyone works better that way. I have to fit in my family commitments. I'm old-fashioned enough to think that my family is more important than my work but they're not very demanding. It's sometimes a bit frustrating having to juggle with my time but I manage to do most of what I want to get done somehow or other.

As well as selling my pictures the other facets of my craft work which are occupying my mind just now are exhibitions and teaching. I'm a member of the Quilters' Guild and had some things in their first exhibition four or five years ago. It's handy to know what's going on, what's happening in the quilting world, and they send me their magazine four times a year. I still make patchwork wall-hangings from time to time, mainly for exhibition purposes. I have one of my own planned for 1985, sharing gallery space with two painters whose work I admire, and I'm working towards that. But for me patchwork comes second — embroidery first. I find it very useful to be a member of the Embroiderers' Guild. I can use their library and study aids, and I buy *Embroidery* magazine.

Very soon I'm having a student coming from America to learn embroidery. The Association of British Craftsmen organise holidays in this country for students from overseas. They are taught by craftspeople on a one-to-one basis, and stay in the home of the tutor for a week or two as one of the family. I have to make myself available to my student for four hours' teaching each day, to take her around to museums and exhibitions, to introduce her to other craftspeople, that sort of thing, and I will be paid quite well for that. It's something new, quite exciting. A challenge.

LIBBY CALVERT
Patchwork Bedspreads

Patchwork bedspreads are my thing. Patchwork with a difference in that I start at the centre, with a picture, then I frame that with material, work round it, frame it again. My design is quite original and began in an interesting way, through a lovely Victorian bedspread owned by my great-aunt. My mother copied it in silk, so she gave me the idea and then I made my own, in cotton. I started with cotspreads and then went on to bedspreads. You could say I was inspired by my mother, but basically I am self-taught.

I just played around with patchwork for quite a long time but I've been doing it seriously for about twelve years or more. It's been my primary job since I was divorced in 1972. I needed to earn some money and I had two young sons so this seemed the ideal sort of work. Something I could do at home in my own time while I was bringing up the boys. So far I've sold the bedspreads on an individual basis, to commission. First I sold to local people, then they told other people and the whole thing spread by word of mouth. I've been very lucky in that my work

LIBBY CALVERT
MARSH COTTAGE
ASTON, OXFORD, OX8 2DQ
TEL. BAMPTON CASTLE (0993) 850658

BEDSPREADS
original patchwork designs

got noticed and talked about and I've had a lot of coverage in the newspapers. In *The Times*, Saturday's *Financial Times*, and the *Sunday Telegraph*, and in local papers, too. I'm quite well known in the area where I live because I organise exhibitions at the local arts centre. That began in 1975 — a 'Rich and Rare' exhibition put on by the West Oxfordshire Arts Association at Bampton — and since then I've done six more. I don't always exhibit in them myself but once when I did, *The Times* did a piece about 'Rich and Rare' and the article began with comment about my bedspreads. That was very helpful, much more so than advertising. What I'd *love* is a full-page feature in *Interiors* which is by far and away the best of all the magazines that are to do with design. That is the one magazine that I buy. I look at *Ideal Home* and *Homes and Gardens,* things like that, but I don't think any of them are as good as *Interiors* for my sort of thing.

I'm a member of the Quilters' Guild which covers both quilting and patchwork though they are really quite different crafts, and I had a bedspread in their second exhibition in 1984. That's quite useful because their exhibitions travel around the country so your work is seen by lots of people in lots of places, and illustrated in full colour in the catalogue. I'm rather different from a lot of other guild members in that I like to work on my own. Very often groups of women make quilts and bedspreads together — it's a communal thing, a shared experience. A lot of quilt-makers like that, but I prefer to do it by myself. The guild magazine is very helpful in that it tells you where to get fabrics.

When I first began patchwork I just used what material I had to get started — that's the way they used to make patchwork bedspreads, using up bits of material. But now the idea is to use new materials, very pretty prints, with a pretty blend of colours. I try to get my bedspread orders in January because that's when the new materials come into the shops, the pretty cotton prints that I need. When I'm commissioned my customer gives me snippets of things from the bedroom so that I can match them up. It might be a scrap of wallpaper or a little piece of curtain material, something like that. Then I take those around and hunt for the fabrics I need. I adore doing that. That's the fun bit. I buy material everywhere, absolutely everywhere, and a lot from John Lewis.

I don't plan the finished look of the bedspread before I begin — the materials themselves dictate the design as I go along. It's not so much like drawing as designing with blocks of colour. There's a lot of geometry involved, a lot of measuring and calculating, because the corners must be perfect. I think there is a change in taste coming in at the moment. The pretty-pretty Laura Ashley look may be going out. The buyers are looking for stark designs in plain colours. Very dramatic. In Harrods they are thinking ahead to red, black and white bedrooms instead of the delicate pastel shades. They asked me if I'd like to have a go at making a bedspread in those colours and I've just finished it. It *is* stark, but it's gorgeous. I'm very pleased with it.

I love making patchwork cushions, too, because I like a change. I make two sizes, 16 inch square and 12 inch square. All filled with feathers, which I buy from the Frome Feather Company. It's such fun tracking down these places. The small cushions are scented, and I buy my pot-pourri from Madelon Baillieu, in Cumbria. I had to find polythene bags, too, for packaging, but you ring around and people pass names on to you. The feather people at Frome helped me to find bags. I enjoyed that — they're all so helpful.

My cushions don't sell particularly well from craft stalls. I think they're too expensive for that. People just don't carry around a lot of money for impulse buying. I find fixing a price for the things I make is very difficult. Whatever you decide some people say it's too much and some people say it's too little. The bedspread I had in the Quilters' Guild exhibition was only half the price of any of the others on show. So it's very random. In the end it comes down to what people will pay. I always sell to shops, a dozen cushions at a time, and we agree on a price that suits us both. You have to choose your shops carefully. Peter Jones is my best customer, and the buyer said, 'We do like your things, they're so up-market.' I thought, 'That's a good word, "up-market". I'll stick to that.' So I always aim for up-market stores, and I sell to Liberty's, John Lewis, and lots of others. Harrods had some for Christmas.

I'm quite brash about selling. I don't ring up and try to make an appointment because then they say, 'What *exactly* do you make?', and my things are so difficult to describe. I just walk in, with a cushion in a carrier bag, and then I pull it out with a flourish and say, 'I want you to look at *this.*' Very brash, really. It helps if you can find out beforehand who to go and see. Occasionally people you meet have contacts and give you useful names. But when I went to Harrods I had no idea and as it happened it was great fun. I started off in one department and the girl there was awfully nice and said, 'No, I think you should try such-and-such a department,' and took me along with her, and then I got passed on again and again, with everybody joining in and taking an interest until at last I got to the right place. It was all rather funny and friendly, a lovely day — and they gave me a big order in the end.

It's very satisfying. Really, a lovely way of life, to make something pretty that other people think pretty. And then to be able to go out and work in the vegetable garden if you feel like it.

WENDY BURTON
'Wendy Beatrix Designs'

I trade under the name Wendy Beatrix Designs, making patchwork and appliqué clothes, mainly dresses and jackets. I also make cot quilts, wall-hangings and cushions to order.

A few years ago, due to my husband's job, I moved to East Grinstead and in order to get to know some people I joined the National House-wives Register. This was a marvellous group and through it I met a girl who made patchwork and, like me, wanted an outlet for selling. We both hated the idea of selling to shops which necessarily had to put such a high mark-up on goods. We wanted to sell items that were a bit different, direct to people who would appreciate them, and at a price they could afford.

Apart from O-level Needlework I had no training, just a natural bent that way. I left school after O-levels, due to family necessity, to work in the Inland Revenue — as a Tax Officer! According-

ing to my father the Civil Service was a very secure and proper place to work. I made most of my own clothes simply because I found it easy and I wanted something different from chain-store clothes. And so I continued through marriage and children until I joined the NHR.

We had no idea about how to get help in setting up a business. We just thought of the cheapest way to reach the public and that was the local market. We had in the meantime roped in two or three other NHR crafty members who agreed to join us in our endeavour, and so we booked our stall. The market was held weekly on Saturdays and was really rather small and grotty — but it was cheap. Our first stall was outside and we soon realised the problems of wind and weather. We had to buy clothes pegs to pin things down! Eventually we moved to an inside stall — disused cattle pens — which we lined with polythene to keep out draughts and rain. This made lighting a necessity so as a group we clubbed together and bought some spot-lights.

Basket of Flowers, Pieced Dress with Appliqué Detail.

WENDY BEATRIX DESIGNS
Patchwork and Appliqué

Wendy Beatrix Designs offer original patchwork and appliqué clothes for adults and children. Natural fabrics are used and colour co-ordination is the main feature. Jackets are quilted and fully lined and all garments are finished to the highest standard. The clothes have appeared in a number of national magazines and are soon to be featured in a book. Each garment is unique and prices are very competitive, starting from £25 for waistcoats and dresses and £45 for jackets. Special commissions are undertaken and have included wallhangings, cushions and quilts.

Oak House, New Road, Wallingford, Oxford
OX10 0AU Telephone Wallingford (0491) 36200

We called the group 'The Ashdown Artisans' which we thought had a tone of quality, and we had regular meetings at which we sorted out any problems and worked out a rota. We also had printed labels made to put on all the garments. The group was limited to six and we all manned the stall, a day at a time. We each gave a set percentage of our takings to the group to pay for the rent and the other expenses so those who sold most paid most into the fund. This helped members who were not selling very well but who were taking a turn manning the stall. We all took a turn doing the books so no one had to give too much time to it. Our clientele built up and people came to look for us having seen us featured in magazines and local papers. This was publicity of our own making. We wrote to magazines, newspapers and even the BBC to tell them about ourselves. All of them responded and we were featured on Radio 4 and Woman's Hour. Being a group gave each of us confidence and we weren't tied to a stall every week. I must add that the other stall holders were very kind and supportive, though secretly, I'm sure, they thought we wouldn't last. We were teased but it was all in good fun and they soon took us seriously when we turned up week after week.

After three years my husband's work meant we had to move to Oxfordshire, so I had to leave the group and consider how I wanted to sell my work in the future. I saw an article about the newly formed Oxfordshire Guild of Craftsmen, and wrote off to join — I am now guild secretary. Through meeting up with other craftspeople I was able to find out about craft fairs, etc, and found my fellow members very helpful and communicative. In my first year I tried many craft fairs but soon learned which were the quality ones and decided to stick to one or two select ones and build up stock towards those. Through the craft fairs I was approached by shop owners who now buy from me direct and keep me going without my having to attend the fairs, but I still show work to the public through guild exhibitions.

As far as standards are concerned I feel it is very important to finish off each garment properly inside — many customers have remarked on this. All seams are folded and stitched, waistbands are bound with braid, and all bodices are lined. I have my own labels printed. This doesn't cost a great deal and it gives a garment a professional look. All my work is done on a domestic sewing-machine. Fabrics are purchased anywhere I see them. I don't want the wholesale minimum of a complete roll of each fabric. I boast that each dress I make is in some way different from all the others so I stick to small amounts of differing fabrics. I do, however, always buy 100 per cent cotton as I prefer to work with natural materials. I started with no capital. I had always sewn so I had some fabric to start with and as soon as I sold something I used the money I earned to buy more fabric so I built up a large stock — of course, this is easier when you're doing patchwork. I love fashion magazines and buy quite a number. This keeps me up to date and gives me some ideas but I must admit, my dresses and jackets are still the same basic design they were when I started. The styles just evolved. They need no buttons or zips since they have to be put in perfectly to look good.

I price my goods at what I think the market will bear. If you underprice to start with it is difficult to put the price up afterwards. It's easier to price high, then to bring the price down if necessary. A guideline is the cost of materials, plus labour at £x an hour minimum, and extra if necessary to bring it up to market price. This doesn't always work as you may have to give shops a discount for quantity. I would advise people not to agree to sale-or-return as you have no control over how the goods are displayed or looked after.

When I first began, at East Grinstead, I needed a long-suffering family since it involved being at the market some weekends. Husbands were very helpful, setting up the stall and taking it down, bringing cars to load with all the goods, etc. It would have been difficult without their support. We used to give them an annual thank-you party in recognition of all they had done for the group. A drawback of craft work is that it is solitary, which is why it is nice to join a guild and meet up with others in the same position. Some people opt for combined workshops with others

to overcome this.

For me there are three main pleasures:

> Making what you like at a pace you like. You can take the afternoon off to sit in the garden if the sun is shining!
> Craft fairs and selling direct to people who are very appreciative — that's very ego-boosting.
> And the craftspeople — they're so very helpful and encouraging.

I make only the quantity of goods I can cope with and work approximately from 10am until 4pm — but not every day and hardly ever at weekends. This is purely personal. I could expand, but I prefer things as they are. I think the enjoyment would go if I had to make too many garments, and I like to have time to make one-off exhibition pieces.

The main personal qualities you require are confidence and patience. Confidence in what you produce. You should never undersell your goods to customers just because you find something easy to make. Not everyone does. And patience. Your business is not likely to take off straight away. Try building up some stock and selling party plan at friends' homes. You need quite a lot of stock to fill up a stall or stand — that's why it is a good idea to team up with someone or a few others to start with. It's nice to remember that Laura Ashley began by printing tea towels on the kitchen table!

JO PALMER
Dress Designer
'The Dream Factory'

It's really quite an extraordinary story, how The Dream Factory began. I was out of work, on the dole, living in Reading. My children were growing up and beginning to leave home and I was earning bits and pieces by doing odd dressmaking jobs. I decided to put my house on the market because it was too big, and make a new start. Some people came to look over my place, liked it, said they wanted it, realised — because of all the pins and things lying all over — that I was a dressmaker, and asked me what I was

going to *do*. 'No idea,' I said. 'Haven't sorted that one out yet.' Then they told me that where they came from, in Painswick, there was a girl doing work just like mine, the same sort of things. We should get together, they said. Well, the upshot was, we exchanged houses. They bought mine and I came to live in theirs, here in Painswick. I'd never even been here, knew nothing at all about it. But that's what happened, and the girl became my partner. It was absolutely fantastic. We got on, just like that. We even shared the same birthday! We totally complemented each other. She had all the skills I didn't have. She'd worked in the theatre, at the Royal Court and places like that, but she hadn't had a proper job for fifteen

Wedding dresses
Evening dresses ; suits ; dresses ; skirts ; jackets

Individual designs, hand-made to order
Pure silks and quality fabrics
Ready-to-wear Bridal range

The Dream Factory, Friday Street, Painswick, Glos. Tel.:(0452)812379 Proprietor : Jo Palmer

years because of her kids. But she had great talent. A really professional attitude. She was marvellous to work with.

My background was totally different to hers. When I left school in 1957 I went to the Benson School of Pattern Cutting and Dressmaking in Baker Street, London, and I learnt to make patterns, which is what I most wanted to do. Cutting is *vital*. That's *the* thing. I did a year there, then I went as an apprentice to two couture-trained dressmakers for two years. That's not often done now, but it was wonderful training. You learnt everything. From there I went on to work as a dress hand for Worth's in Grosvenor Street. In the late fifties it was still all hopping. They were making clothes properly. To work in a fitting-room like that was amazing, great experience. When I started having my children I had to freelance from home, but as soon as they were old enough I went to the London College of Fashion and learnt about mass production. Totally different from couture, of course, but very important. And then, *then* I worked in a factory as a pattern machinist making skirts. That was real work, probably the most useful thing I ever did. They don't know what it's like nowadays. I started at 7.30, had 10 minutes, *10 minutes,* for coffee, that's all, and ½ hour for lunch. We

couldn't talk, there was no talk, it was so noisy. It was just 'Eyes down, baby, and get on with it.' We finished at 4.30. A hell of a long day, you know!

So that was it, more or less, until we started The Dream Factory. The name came from my partner. Her son was reading *Charlie and the Chocolate Factory* at the time, and we were in the business of dreams — very romantic, beautiful clothes, wonderful fabrics, dreamy styles. Fantasy dresses for special occasions. The amazing thing was, we didn't need any money to start. We worked from my home and we just had an ordinary sewing-machine each. The customers brought their own materials, and they paid us before they took the clothes away. A lot of people have material, you know. Often they've had it tucked away for ages. They present you with it and say, 'What am I to do with this?' Then we put our heads together and draw something. I'm no good at drawing, but they do a lot of it for you, and together we work out a design. Even today I get the money before the clothes leave the shop. It's a good business to be in because you don't get caught. No one gets a garment until it's been paid for. I sometimes take a

Plate 7 Carpet bags and tapestry bags from Harrick Hart Carpet Bags

cheque before it's been cleared but I laugh and say, 'If this one bounces I'll put your name up in my window!' It's just a joke, of course — but anyway, it's never happened. I only had trouble once. I made a garment, exactly what the customer wanted. She came to collect it and she was thrilled, delighted. Then she took it home and obviously her husband didn't like it because back she came — the fabric was all wrong, the style wasn't right, it wasn't what she had hoped . . . In the end we just charged her for the material, lost the cost of our labour.

Sadly, after a couple of years, the partnership fizzled out for various reasons. I kept going on my own and it's just gone on, thank God. I'm hoping to expand my premises soon, but at present I work from two rooms. One is a combined fitting- and show-room, with a window on to the street where I can put one lovely frock on display. It has a rail of clothes, some for sale, some special orders. And lovely design drawings of my range that an artist friend did for me, and photographs of some of the weddings that I have dressed. That's the room where the business is done. The other room is my work-room, where I make the clothes and store my fabrics. I keep my sewing-machine there — an industrial Singer which is absolutely marvellous, so heavy and sturdy that no one who has used one would go back to a domestic model, because they're so light, and slip around all over the place. This one is fantastically quick, and it will sew anything, any material from denim to crêpe de chine. My other marvellous machine, which is absolutely vital, is an overlocker. I couldn't do without that. Then I have a *large* table, topped with Formica, for cutting out, and it has drawers at either side, for storage. A dressmaker's dummy, an iron, and an ironing-board with an extension for doing sleeves. That's about it. Lots of shelves and cupboards and boxes and bags, of course. The place looks a mess but I try to keep it tidy

Plate 8 (top) Patchwork bedspread from Libby Calvert (*The Quilter's Guild*); (bottom) Grey striped jumper from Cathie McKnight; train jumper and wool from one of Dorothy Greenwood's Knit-In knitting packs; hairdresser's jumpsuit from Ann Wright, Gasper; glove puppets from Jan Burrage, The Gables Workshop

and I always know exactly where everything is.

I need lots of light, and lots of heat. That's important. One gets very cold, staying still and concentrating hard, and I must be warm and comfortable to work well.

I don't do much advertising because it costs a fortune, but if you work out a little press release, a photograph or drawing with a bit of spiel, and send it off to an up-market magazine, you can sometimes get in as a feature. We sent off a drawing and some spiel to *Vogue* magazine and they rang up and said, 'Yes, that's lovely', and put it in, and people came from miles, Scotland, Cardiff and Norfolk, to order special clothes. You do need to show off what you make with good photographs. The trouble is, it costs a bomb, but I've decided it's got to be done. I'm working on a display stand now. It will have photographs of the clothes being made, and of the finished product, swatches of material, and free advertising stuff, brochures, leaflets, that sort of thing. And I'll have a dummy with a dress on it to one side. I'll use that at wedding festivals. A lot of hotels round here put those on. They bring to-

White satin w/coat & underskirt
(poss. simple strapless dress)
spotted voile blouse with
frilled ribbon neck and voile
overskirt with large frill.

labels, brochures, and so on, all with the Dream Factory logo. And the clothes themselves are beautiful. I really adore lovely fabrics, wonderful textures, velvets, silks, lace. Most of them I buy from Germany where it's amazing — they'll let you have a minimum of only 8 metres on wholesale terms. You can't do that in England. But I do buy from London-based manufacturers, too, and from John Lewis if I only need a small quantity.

I've never needed to borrow money for the business, but I have an overdraft facility, just in case I might need it. A friend showed me how to keep my own books, and once a year I send them off to an accountant for an annual audit, and to get them ready for the tax man.

I don't know exactly how I cost my work — I suppose I reckon on what people can manage, whatever seems reasonable. I use two outworkers, but I'd really like to have one of those government trainees from the Youth Training Scheme because that's just like the old idea of an apprentice, isn't it? So — I calculate the outworkers' wages, and the cost of material, and £5 an hour for myself . . . and then I stick something on top of that. I just know what my clothes are worth, I suppose, because I've been in the rag trade all my life.

I make wedding dresses and special occasion clothes because that's where the money is, that's what people will pay for. And because you can fantasise more. But I do anything — put in a zip for the local butcher, make a tweed skirt for a little old lady. I like making special dresses, but I'll tell you something — it's lovely having a little old lady who's a really weird shape, and she has her own special occasion coming up. If you can make her something that she feels good in, feels really lovely in, better than she's ever done, because it's *right*, and it fits properly — that's terribly exciting. I like making dresses for real people, dresses that the person can shine through, not get smothered by. I love the business of talking to the customers, finding out how they see themselves, how they think about themselves, what they are really like, what they really want — and then making their dreams come true. The dream factory — that's the pleasure.

gether all the people who do wedding things — dressmakers, hire firms, cake-makers, florists, photographers, printers, holiday organisers, and so on — and we can all chat to interested customers, show them what we do and talk about costs.

The other event which will be a new venture for me is taking part in an exhibition put on by the Gloucestershire Guild of Craftsmen. It's a prestige thing, really. I've just become a member and I find people are quite impressed by that. If you can show your things through the guild it's a useful way of getting known and picking up orders.

I always try to present my clothes as beautifully as possible. My husband does printing and art work for advertising — that's his profession — so we have designed the stationery and display material together and I have a lovely range of letter-headings, cards, swing-tickets, sew-in

LADY'S SPOTTED SWEATER

This sweater is fun and easy to knit in any colour combination of your choice.

Measurements
Bust: 90-97cm. (36-38in.)
Actual measurement: 109cm (43in.)
Length from shoulder: 60cm. (23½in.)
Sleeve seam: 47cm. (18½in.)

Materials
7 50g. balls of Phildar Vizir in Bengale, main colour (MC).
2 50g. balls in Ivoiry 1st contrast (A).
2 50g. balls in Ardoise 2nd contrast (B).
1 pair each of 4mm. (No. 8) and 5mm. (No.6) knitting needles.
The quantities of yarn given are based on average requirements and are therefore approximate.

Tension
17 sts. and 25 rows to 10cm. on 5mm. needles over st.st.

Abbreviations
The standard knitting abbreviations are given on the special divider card. We recommend that you keep this by you while working and refer to it when you need to.

N.B. Use separate balls of colour for each motif, and twist colours together at junctions to prevent holes forming.

BACK
With 4mm. needles and MC, cast on 81 sts., and work in rib as follows:
1st row * K.1, P.1, rep. from * to last st., K.1.
2nd row * P.1, K.1, rep. from * to last st., P.1.
Rep. these 2 rows to form the rib and work straight until back measures 9cm. from cast-on edge, ending with a 2nd row, and inc. 12 sts. evenly across this last row. (93 sts.)
Change to 5mm. needles and starting with a K. row, work in st.st. from chart, working K. rows from right to left, and P. rows from left to right.
Cont. working from chart, shaping armholes on 77th row as shown.
Cont. until the 117 rows of chart have been completed.

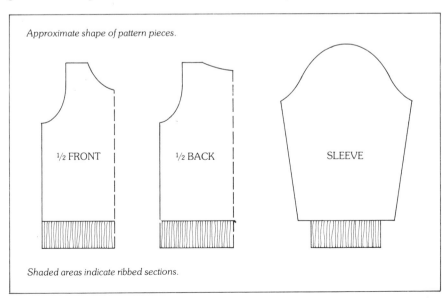

Approximate shape of pattern pieces.

½ FRONT ½ BACK SLEEVE

Shaded areas indicate ribbed sections.

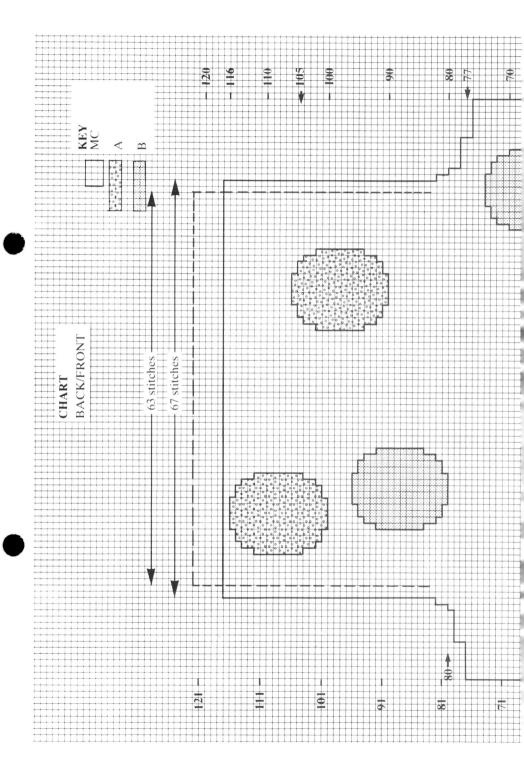

CHART
BACK/FRONT

KEY
MC
A
B

63 stitches
67 stitches

120
116
110
105
100
90
80
77
70

121
111
101
91
81
80
71

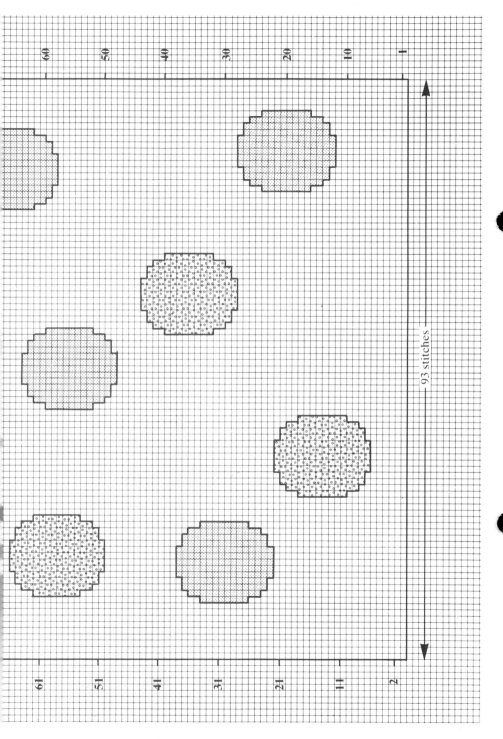

Designed by Sylvie Faundris. Photo Bettina Reims with Elisabeth Jéau, Murielle Alain

93 stitches

MARILYN BECKER
Ribbon Weaver
'Ribbon Designs'

I didn't begin working with ribbons until three or four years ago. I never used to think of myself as particularly artistic or creative, though I did embroidery as a hobby. But now I believe it was a latent talent, always there, just waiting for something to trigger it off, waiting to find an outlet. The trigger came a few years ago when I saw ribbon weaving at an exhibition, and I was entranced by it. It all started from there. I had to teach myself because there are hardly any books on the subject. I couldn't find any, but now there is a pamphlet available, with a few basic designs. I taught myself by trial and error, once I'd had a good look at it and studied it carefully in the exhibition. It's never been really recognised as a separate craft. In Victorian days it was just considered something that needlewomen did almost automatically, part of their lives.

I liked it because it was quick and effective. And so varied. You can be dramatic, delicate, romantic, practical. It's the actual working out that takes the time — working out where to place the ribbons. Once you've figured out how to do it the first time it's quite quick to do it again. I keep a portfolio of all the things I've done, as a record.

The first thing I made was a little cushion. Then I made more. I've always worked with my husband in the curtain business. He's in retail, and I'm involved on the selling side, with the customers. So I did some cushions and sold them in our shop. People seemed to like them, so I went on from there to exhibit in the Living Crafts Fair, at Hatfield House. It was still just cushions at that stage. Then people began asking me how it was done, but I didn't really want to tell them because I'd found it all out for myself, the hard way. So the next year I went along to Hatfield House with a new idea. My brother drew some illustrations of my weaving, and I wrote out instructions, had them nicely photocopied, and sold the instruction sets for 50p. They included the basics of ribbon weaving technique, plus step-by-step guidance for three different designs.

By now I was getting more and more successful, and I did an exhibition at Camden Arts Centre. It was the same as at Hatfield House, you had to be chosen to exhibit. Your work had to be up to a certain standard. It was very satisfying to pass the test because I was still new and nervous. I felt it was a great accolade to be accepted. In fact, any craft fair which accepts work that hasn't even been seen hasn't got a high standard of craftsmanship. There should be some sort of selection, or they end up with a lot of rubbish and the customers don't know what to expect.

When I discovered that customers actually wanted to do ribbon weaving for themselves, not necessarily to buy the finished article, I had the idea of producing ribbon kits. I now have three kits that I sell. The first was for a very simple cushion, the second was a more complicated cushion with a 'tumbling blocks' design, and the new one that I've just brought out is for an evening bag. Presentation of kits is very important. I've seen some that have everything just jumbled up together in a polythene bag, but that's not good enough. I don't think so, anyway. I pack mine so that people can see exactly what they're buying, and the colours of the ribbons. And there's a good photograph to show what it will look like when it's finished. It was a very difficult business, getting the kits organised. I do all my own designing, and all my own packaging. I had to find a printer, and then I had to find the actual packaging materials, the plastic bags and the cardboard inners. That was very frustrating. It took me a year to get the kits on to the market, thousands of phone calls, miles of foot-slogging. The sellers want to sell you hundreds of thousands of bags or wrappers, and I can't cope with those sorts of numbers although I do pay more through buying small quantities.

I had the same sort of problem recently when I was trying to buy a display stand. People are not helpful unless you're in the business of fitting out about ten shops with miles of shelving. I just rang my way through the *Yellow Pages*, asking

---

Ribbon Designs
42 Lake View, Edgware, Middx. HA8.7RU.

people, describing what I wanted, and at last I found a company which is absolutely super to deal with. What I said was, I know I'm small but help me now and perhaps we can grow big together.

I sell mostly at craft shows, and through repeat orders to people who have bought from me before, and to some West End shops. I find it quite easy to get a mention in magazines if I send them information. I'm just putting out some blurb about my evening bag kit now. My work was mentioned in *Ideal Home* when they wrote up 'Living Crafts', then *Homes and Gardens* did a feature for which they visited shops like ours throughout the country. They happened to notice my kits and gave them a little mention, and there was a phenomenal reponse. You have to do your homework properly, keep an eye on the magazines, and see where their interests lie. I noticed that *Woman's Realm* was very interested in craft work so I sent them a cushion and they gave it a little mention and now I've just taken them a bedspread and some cushions. They're going to do a whole feature, showing how you can buy four cushion kits and turn them into a bedspread, and they'll say where to send for the kits. That could keep me busy. I don't know what the response will be but I could cope with a lot of orders because I have about half a dozen outworkers I can call on. It's very useful to have them on tap, though I really prefer to do the work myself. I do a little bit of advertising in *Popular Crafts* and *Crafts and Leisure,* and in *Embroidery,* which is the magazine of the Embroiderers' Guild, because I'm a member of that, but there's not a fantastic response. Editorial comment is worth much more if you can get it, and I do, I suppose, because I'm making something totally different and novel. I cottoned on to this quite quickly. I saw that little publication called *Home & Freezer Digest* which is a sort of home market place which finds its way into thousands of homes and it has a crafts page. I wrote to them and they took me on. A full page. I had to give away some hints but it was worth it. When you think of the price of having a full-page advertisement in a national magazine — it would cost a fortune.

I've just done my first teaching session — that's another way of making cash from crafts. I saw the nearby arts centre mentioned in our local paper and I thought — well, there might be something there for me. So I contacted the Director and showed her my work, and she gave me a full morning workshop as a result. That was a great success so I'm going back in a few months to do a whole day.

The main problems I come up against are not being able to buy in sufficient quantities to get good competitive prices and satisfactory service from the suppliers, and having to spend so much time on things like organising the details and getting the packaging done, and making sure the presentation is right. Recently I've been exercising my mind over producing an all-white cushion because I've been asked for one over and over again. But the problem of tracking down all the ribbons in various shades of white, and getting the cushion drawn and well photographed has beaten me so far, even though there is a demand. Thank goodness I've recently found a studio able to photograph my things well, and at a reasonable price.

What I *like* is getting ideas, and producing them. One of my first ideas was for a ribbon bedspread, all in cream, made from satin, velvet and lace. A great variety of shades and textures. It took an amazing amount of leg-work to find all the materials to match, but the result was well worth it. It's quite beautiful. I wove the squares and patched them together, and my outworkers did the machining, lining and finishing. I have great hopes of selling it to Liberty's or somewhere like that, but in a way I'll be sad because I'm so very fond of it.

Ribbon weaving hasn't got enormous commercial application since ribbons are expensive — they've gone up in price enormously during the last two years. Also it's a labour-intensive craft. I don't think anybody has found a machine that can do it. It has to be hand-made. For one cushion the ribbons alone would cost about £3 before one takes account of edging, vilene, backing satin, and so on, so they can't be cheap. I fix my prices by a very hit-and-miss method. It's easy to cost the materials, but difficult to price one's labour. I just have a good idea of what's right, and always bear in mind that a shop will pay me much less than I would get if I sold the same article privately because it has to put on a huge margin for overheads.

I love the work. I'd like to spend nine-tenths of my time with ribbons, but I have to remember that I'm a wife and mother as well as having my duties in the shop. It's difficult, getting through it all, and sometimes I get very frustrated, but there are such rewards. The love of the craft carries me through. And the high spots — like having one of the cushions accepted as a gift for the royal wedding and going on show with all the other wedding presents. That was wonderful.

JAN BURRAGE
Puppet-maker
'The Gables Workshop'

It's rather unusual to make puppets for a living, a difficult job to explain. When people ask us what we do we tend to say 'Self-employed'! It began years ago when my husband Ralph was in the Air Force. There was a two-yearly exhibition called 'RAF-EX', and we both used to do oil paintings and put them in for that, and we always won prizes and certificates. Then someone said, 'It's all right for you, you can paint. I bet you couldn't do anything else and win a prize.' Well — I took on the bet. It *was* 3 o'clock in the morning at a mess 'do'! I went home and waded through about twenty categories of arts and crafts and thought, 'Oh, I couldn't *do* any of these,' and then I hit on toymaking. 'Surely I could make toys,' I thought. I used to make them for my children, and for the nursery school I ran for RAF children. So I thought I'd try to make a puppet, and I started playing about with two cone shapes. I tried them all ways and the inspiration wouldn't come. Then my husband just changed the angle, twisted them around, and there we had it — the first puppet. It just came to life like that. We called her Mrs Murey because she was so demure, with closed eyes and huge, hand-made eyelashes. She was the first puppet we ever made — we still have her — and she won an award in 'RAF-EX'. We actually got a first with her and won some real money instead of just a certificate. Then she was used in an RAF recruiting centre exhibition.

That was the beginning. We just sold to friends in the first place. Then we thought of someone we knew who had a little shop in Stow-on-the-Wold. Ralph said, 'Why don't we take a puppet along just to show her, find out what she thinks?' — and she wanted to buy it. Then she rang and said could she have six more, please, as soon as possible, because it had only been in the window ten minutes before it was sold. It was a real scramble to make six. Up till then I'd been doing one at a time. That was my first lesson — always make more than one, it saves hours if you make a few together.

My puppets started as a hobby but our lives were changed completely three and a half years ago. My husband had left the Air Force and had another job — then suddenly he was made redundant. We sat down and thought what we could do and decided to try to make the hobby into a business. Our family was off our hands so we just had ourselves to worry about and we thought it was a chance we'd regret not taking. It was a challenge, a hell of a gamble, but we had our own house and it was too big for us, so that helped. Rather than move into a smaller place we got planning permission from the local council to turn one big bedroom into a workshop, and got busy. Things have gone so well that now we're moving into a new workshop attached to the house, so that we can expand. We like working from home. We've always thought that a factory situation would ruin the cottage industry idea.

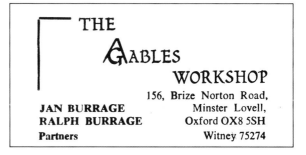

THE

ᴀGABLES

WORKSHOP

156, Brize Norton Road,

JAN BURRAGE   Minster Lovell,

RALPH BURRAGE   Oxford OX8 5SH

Partners   Witney 75274

We used my husband's redundancy money to launch the business, and called it The Gables Workshop because our house was called The Gables. Afterwards, when it was too late, we discovered that we could have applied to Witney Council and got a grant of £2,000 to set up, but we didn't know that then. We just struggled along on our own money. My husband could have gone on the dole, but he didn't. We used our own resources. The only thing we've needed to borrow money for is to build the new extension, and that's an investment because it will improve our productivity. Give us more space and make our time-and-motion more economical.

After three-and-a-half years we have no regrets. I see my husband five days a week instead of two, the way most women do, and we have a good partnership. Our weeks are inside out. He's at home on weekdays, but away selling our things at the weekends, at the Jubilee Market in Covent Garden. You have to find out the best places to sell. We've had a stand at the British Toy and Hobby Fair at Earls Court, and picked up orders and sold to shops in Oxford Street and Regent Street and places like that, but we didn't particularly care for that way of selling. You get pressured. Day after day, making things that other people want you to make instead of what *you* want to make. There's no time to develop new ideas, they keep slipping ahead, getting delayed. A beefburger manufacturer asked us to make thirty thousand puppets for his firm, but of course we couldn't take that on. It was far too big for a business the size of ours. Still, it was nice to be asked.

We tried selling from lots of places, and in the end we decided to make Covent Garden our main outlet. It's right for us — though it may seem a long way to go from Oxford each week. It attracts a lot of people, it has the right atmosphere, and the organisation is of the highest quality.

There are many craft fairs and craft markets, and it is up to the individual craftsperson to choose the ones to suit themselves, but they cannot get any idea of the type of market until they have tried them. There are good days and bad days — and the bad days have to be put down to experience. A craft market stall is your 'shop window' and unless you show an interest in your goods and customers, those customers will show little interest in you.

Covent Garden is so good because it attracts big crowds, and lots of people from abroad. We have buyers from America coming for our puppets, and recently there have been enquiries from France.

As far as our business is concerned, my husband does the organising and marketing. I could never really believe that I could make anything that people would want to buy. He's the one who has confidence in me. He can always sell as much as I can make. I think that's good, because it's difficult to sell your own things, push yourself forward. I do the designing and the making. There are just the two of us in the partnership, with four outworkers to help. I don't really like to call them 'outworkers' though. We don't just make puppets, we make fun, and the fun seems to rub off: Our helpers really seem to enjoy what they're making.

Originally I trained as a commercial artist and I've put that skill into creating the puppets. I go from Z to A. I see the finished product and work backwards, start with the actual shapes, and then make my own patterns. We try always to be original and funny, play games with ideas and words. For instance, we make a worm-shaped ring that we call a 'Ring-worm', and a worm book-mark that is our 'Book-worm'. That was my husband's idea, and he's very proud of it! Another good idea happened just by chance. I made some little, colourful, furry maggots, and Ralph said, 'I need something like an apple to display them on.' So we made a wooden board shaped like an apple and that caused an enormous amount of interest. In the end, we turned it into a maggot puzzle. The apple is full of maggot holes, all different colours, and each maggot has to be popped into the hole that is the same colour as it is.

Mostly we make puppets, though, in vividly coloured felt or fur fabric. Finger puppets, glove puppets, and huge squeaky puppets that people hang round their necks — Squeaky Cedrics, we call them. Sadly, we've just lost our fabric supply for those, it's not going to be imported any longer and we can't find a good alternative material so we'll have to stop production of that line. Our favourite, and our best seller, is our tortoise. He has a number on his back because he's a marathon tortoise — just coming in from last year's marathon.

Although we really make for children, and have a group of children to try our ideas on, 70 per cent of our puppets go to adults. They buy them for children then they come back and say, 'Er . . . can I have another one please? The last one I bought as a present but I'm afraid I kept it for myself.'

Everything we know now we've had to find out for ourselves, through experience, trial and error. We knew from the beginning that we had to observe safety regulations but we had great difficulty in finding out about them. In the end we went to the Citizens' Advice Bureau and there were masses of pamphlets and leaflets to wade through. As far as finding out where to buy fabrics, well, every professional craftsman worth his salt knows about the International Craft and Hobby Fair at Wembley every year. It's a wonderful source for materials, you can make all the contacts you want. But since this is a *trade* fair it's not open to the general public. Now I buy from Brimlakes — fur fabric in 40-metre rolls! When I think how I started, saving a little bit out of the housekeeping to buy sufficient material to make the next puppet!

You *can* make a go of a craft business provided that you are prepared to work hard, find things out, and get on with it. Make something that you like, that you know you can sell, and search out the right place to sell it. One last thought — we have, over the years of designing, making and selling, made many mistakes, but we never make the same mistakes twice!

CATHIE McKNIGHT
Knitwear

Basically, I make hand-framed jerseys and cardigans. They may be thick and woolly and warm or they may be made from cotton and look more like tee-shirts, but basically they're all jerseys and cardigans. And I make one or two dresses as well.

About six years ago I borrowed a friend's knitting-machine for a month or so and had a go on it to try it out, then a couple of years later I borrowed my mother-in-law's and played about with that. I was obviously keen because when I returned my mother-in-law's I borrowed one from another friend and enjoyed it so much that I enrolled for adult education classes in machine-knitting, held locally. Unfortunately, I only managed to keep that up for three or four months because I developed glandular fever and was ill for quite a while. Then eighteen months ago I decided at last to take it seriously, and bought myself a Knitmaster Electronic. Since then I've been knitting regularly but it has to be part-time because I have three children to look after, and a busy life.

To start with friends and family asked me to make them things, then people would see something I was wearing and say, 'Oh, I wish you'd make me one like that.' When I began I was looking upon it purely as a hobby. I'd never have dreamed that I would ever consider it as anything else. But now things have changed. My marriage has broken up and I'm having to look around for ways to make proper money. I got off to quite a good start because I have a lot of well-to-do friends who thought nothing of paying me £30, £40, or even £50 for a sweater, but you can't go *on* selling to friends. I've never tried selling to shops because they put on *at least* 100 per cent mark-up and I haven't got the sort of name that would make a shop feel able to price my sweaters at £100 or so — though there are plenty of those around! I recently got involved in party selling for the first time and that was a great success. I also learnt an enormous number of useful lessons from it. I teamed up with two friends and we put on two parties, first an evening one, and then a morning one the next day. The first one was pretty useless. We hardly sold anything. It was in a house a long way out of the centre of town and the only people who were prepared to make the trek were good friends anxious to show willing and give moral support. Then the room was very small and we had the knitwear piled on a table in the middle, and once we'd got a dozen people in there nobody could get near enough to have a good look. So they all just crowded together and talked a lot and drank a lot and had a jolly time and bought nothing. The morning party was much better. Much more space to display our things well and more people who were really interested in buying, so we *did* do well out of that and now that I know what the score is I'll do it again.

Up till now my pricing has been pretty random, more or less 'what the market will bear', as they say. If the style is complicated, or more to the point, if it looks complicated, I can charge £50. For a simpler pattern I'll charge £30 to £40. I can't possibly charge according to the hours I put in because I'm still quite new to the knitting world and slower than I should be on my machine. Besides, with three children I never get an uninterrupted hour — it's all bits and pieces here and there. Very difficult to add up and cost out.

I don't buy my yarns at wholesale prices because I never know beforehand what a customer is going to want. Besides, you have to buy such a lot to get a discount. I prefer to buy and make for individuals. I get my wool from Handywoman in Chiswick, and I send off for cottons, by post, to William Hall & Co. It's an old-fashioned firm and they take *weeks* to send anything, but when I saw their advertisement somewhere and sent off for samples I thought their shade card was wonderful, very extensive, much better than anyone else's.

I put labels into all my garments. One says 'Designed and hand-framed by Cathy McKnight' and gives my telephone number. Then I also have a label stating the type of yarn I've used. If you are selling commercially these days you must have a description of the fabric content. Then I have a wash-care label . . . 'Hand-wash only', that's always the safest thing. Three labels in all. I found a label-maker through looking in the small ads at the back of a craft magazine, though I'm afraid I rarely *buy* craft magazines, I

just rummage through them in the newsagent's. I used to get *Fashion Craft* which I found very helpful, and now I look at *Vogue* and *Harpers & Queen* to give me design ideas.

At present I'm still only making pocket money, but I'm deeply involved in exploring ways of turning it into proper money. I've gone back to college and am doing a general course in London at the Central School of Arts and Crafts. I started in February and go once a week for a 2½-hour session. We did two sessions on Knitting Technology — that's really about finding your way round a knitting-machine. Then we did two sessions in the dyeing-room, learning about modern colour techniques. After that we spent a whole term working with the Head of Textiles who taught us how to conceptualise our designs, get the design out of our heads and translate it into wearable garments. It's a wonderful ad hoc course which was created to suit the needs of the class. We were able to decide what we wanted to learn, instead of being told by other people what they thought we needed to know.

The guy who teaches us takes a real interest in our work. He came along to the knitwear party and though he enjoyed it and said lots of nice things about it he thought we were making some mistakes. To start with, he thought we were offering too much choice. He said it would be better to offer fewer designs but to do each one in a range of three colour-ways. Some people were so confused by the choice that they went away empty-handed just because they couldn't make their minds up, so he was probably right there. The other thing he thought was that we should push our garments up-market — get right away from the restrained top-quality Marks & Spencer image into something quite different — so sensational and dramatic that people couldn't resist it.

It's difficult to work out which direction to move in in the future, how to get it *right*, because there's a lot of competition at the moment, masses of people doing the same thing. I'm exploring the possibilities of selling through shops, or through top markets like Covent Garden and Camden Lock because I've been there and seen the customers and watched what they're buying and the sort of money they're spending. There are other possibilities, too. I know an agent who sells to America twice a year and she would handle my goods for a commission. But that's quite a big deal. You have to plan ahead for the next season all the time, and produce masses of stuff well in advance. I've also thought of selling through the Chelsea Arts and Crafts Fair in the autumn. That's a marvellous selling place because lots of foreign buyers come looking for suppliers.

Opportunities of all sorts offer themselves. It's just a question of discovery. But I think the answer is to get your own small basis firmly established first of all, work out exactly what you can do and what you want to do, think it all out very carefully — and *then* you can decide on your direction.

Cathie McKnight
23 Queens Gardens
London W2
Tel: 01-723 0365

LENE BRAGGER
Textile Craftsman
'Hillside Crafts'

I work in all sorts of hand-made textiles: batik and screen printing made up into pictures and wall-hangings; silk and cotton screen-printed smocks and dresses; lamp-shades set with pressed grasses, flowers, ferns and leaves; paper-cuts and mobiles. My most successful line is probably my hand-made, made-to-measure shoes. They are made from cord or quilted silk with batik strips. They have flat rubber soles and are tied over the ankle with laces.

I suppose I am interested in shoes because I take a size 8! I am Danish, and I go back to Denmark every year. Fashions there seem to me to be a bit in advance of the things I see in Britain. About four years ago I saw Chinese slippers, and they looked so pretty and comfortable, but I hadn't seen anything like them here so I had a good look at them and I thought, 'I could make those'.

As far as shoe-making is concerned I'm very fortunate in living in Kendal which is, of course, a big shoe-making centre and the home of K Shoes. There are classes in shoe-making at the local 'tech'. They are really for the workers in the factories to learn to make traditional shoes but I thought I could go along and use the facilities and benefit from them.

To start with the sale of shoes went steadily but slowly, but when I decided to sell through mail order it changed all that. I put a little illus-

trated advertisement in the *Guardian,* describing the three styles I made. I asked people to draw around both feet on a piece of paper and send their footprints with their choice of type and colour, and cheque, to my address. The advertisement went in on an Easter Saturday and I was away for a few days' holiday. When I was on my way home I wondered vaguely whether there'd be any response to the ad but I had no

Handmade shoes
made to measure.

Just draw around both feet on a piece of paper and send it with your choice of type and colour.
Made in either cord or quilted silk with rubber soles, they are strong and very comfy. Tied over ankel with laces and the sole completely flat.
Choose closed toe or open sandal in any 3 types:

1. Cord with roseprint pink, mid-blue or grey.
   £11·50
   p+p included.

2. Cord with silk batik strips pink, mid-blue, grey, navy, wine, green, black, brown **£12·50**

3. Quilted silk with batik strips - any pastel colour **£14·00**

113

size S : 12-14
size L : 16-18
State length required:
26" - 32"

Here .. is a selection of clothes
all handprinted on cotton or pure
silk to order from "Hillside Crafts"

designed by Lene Brøgger
member of Guild of Lakeland Craftsmen

① <u>Dress</u> with handprinted inset on
front and huge pockets.
Dropped waistline, square neck, full skirt.
Loose and comfy.

a. navy cotton with blue, red insets ⎫
b. pale blue cotton with turqoise, mauve ⎬ 29·00
c. pink cotton with lilac, wine ⎭
d. any pastel colour pure silk   £ 38·00

③ <u>Overtunic</u>
in thick cotton, printed.
a. light blue denim
b. apricot denim
c. cream drill
d. bottle green drill
                    £15·00

size m : 32-34"-36"
size L : 38-40"
give chest measurement

All prices include p+p.
28 days delivery
Money back if goods returned
within 7 days.
Please send cheque with address,
details of style, colour & size to:
Hillside Crafts

② <u>Bib-skirt</u>

Wrap around
adjustable size

s-m : 28" length
m-l : 32" length

delicate print

Viyella :
a. mid-blue
b. mid-brown ⎬ 19·50
c. cream

Cord :
d. blue, wine, brown
£24·00

Antung silk :
e. Any pastel colour
to order:
£29·50

④ <u>Shirt :</u>

Printed on yokes,
peasant style with
gathers.
a. cream, Viyella ⎫
b. mid-blue Viyella ⎬ £19·5(
c. pale blue cotton ⎭
d. pink cotton
e. cream cotton
f. any pastel colour
silk -   £25·00

size m. L.
give chest measurement.

idea that it would be so huge. I couldn't push the front door open because of the pile of orders — there were seventy in all! — and even seven or eight months later orders were still coming in from that one advertisement. Strange — people obviously cut it out and put it away and thought about it, and *then* ordered their shoes.

The people who wanted them fell into two groups — young people and students, who were looking for something trendy and special, and people who had a complex about their feet because they were big like mine, or badly shaped. You should have seen some of the footprints I was sent — all sorts of weird and wonderful outlines, bumps and lumps . . . bunions, I suppose! And the letters! You'd be amazed. 'Are you the answer to my long-felt prayer?' one woman wrote. And, 'Your shoes are just what I have been *longing* for!' . . . that sort of thing.

I must say I'm amazed when I go into shoe shops to buy shoes even for my little girl and get presented with pointed toes and all kinds of unsuitable fashions. When I complain about shoes that are offered to me and say they are too narrow I am told, 'Oh, but you shouldn't have let your feet *spread,* Madam, then you could get shoes to fit.' But what *I* think is that shoes should be made to fit feet, not feet forced to fit shoes.

Anyway, there I was with an order for seventy pairs of shoes, and I was legally required to do them all within twenty-eight days. It was no joke. I had to work like mad. I am separated from my husband and my kids are only 8 and 5 so I can't work full-time. I have to push myself really hard between taking them to school and then going to fetch them home again at about 3 pm. I don't usually work much while they're around because I need to spend time with them but after 9 pm, when I've got them to bed and read them their bed-time stories, I manage to put in a few more hours. When I was coping with my deluge of shoes I had to stay at it until about 1 o'clock in the morning, day after day, to get through it all. I did send little friendly hand-written cards to people halfway through saying, 'Sorry, I'm really snowed under but I've got your order and I'll get the shoes to you just as soon as I possibly can', and nobody seemed to mind. I was just worried that I'd promised 28-day delivery — I

think you have to with mail order, I'm not sure — and might be in trouble with the law, or the *Guardian,* if I didn't manage it. I also promised to send their money back if the goods were returned within seven days, but the nice thing was, only two pairs ever came back. That was really reassuring. I had visions of lots of them being sent back, and with all those funny shapes and sizes they'd be quite impossible to sell to anyone else.

The shoes have turned out to be a good money-spinner, and I make about six pairs a week, but I do like to do the other things too. The batik landscape pictures are the most 'me', but they are really hard work so I'd hate to do them all the time, I like being able to change and have variety. The lamp-shades are very popular, and much less demanding, but I'm not so proud of those.

I do some teaching as well. During the summer Lancaster University becomes a sort of intellectual Butlins Holiday Camp, and I've done a fortnight of children's craft classes there, but it was *exhausting.* I had to go away camping after that to recover my energies. I did train as a teacher but I only taught properly for a year because all the time I was teaching I was thinking, 'What I really want to be doing is my craft work', so I gave that up and for ten years now I've been registered as a proper home-based business, Hillside Crafts, with a business bank account, an accountant and outworkers.

I haven't really had what you'd call a formal training. I came to Britain when I was eighteen and got a place at Leeds University to study art, but I couldn't get a student's grant until I'd been resident in this country for three years. I looked around for a private scholarship and approached lots of firms, and Courtaulds said they couldn't give me a scholarship but they could give me a job in their textile department, so I worked for them for a year. Then I married, and moved, and Leeds became impossible, but I've just gone on working, and learning, and picking up the techniques I needed wherever and whenever I could. In Denmark we have a different attitude to arts and crafts, they're more part of everyday life, in a way. We believe you can make *anything* if you just put your mind to it.

Now I'm very involved with the Guild of Lakeland Craftsmen, and put in a lot of hours — perhaps one day a week, though I really haven't got the time — helping on a voluntary basis. I think the Guild is useful and very important. It gives me contact with 200 members. I can sell my work through its permanent gallery above the Sheepskin Centre in Keswick. It stops me from staying at home and getting too involved in doing my own thing, looking inward and becoming introverted and out of touch with what's happening out there. Most of all, it inspires me to do better work. The Guilds are there for the craftsmen but basically, what you get out of them depends upon how much you put in.

I must say I enjoy my life in crafts. It's not a way to get rich. I don't quite pay my way yet, but as I say, I can't work full-time because of the children. And you have to work very very hard, long hours. But I'm my own boss, life is full of variety and every day is different. I'd hate to be in an 'ordinary' job after this.

DOROTHY GREENWOOD
Knitting Pack Designer
'Knit-In'

I studied chemistry, maths and physics at a polytechnic, and when I qualified I worked for Beecham's research laboratory. Then everything changed for me when my husband and I started to foster an 11-year-old boy. I quit my job and decided I'd have to stay at home to look after him properly. I cast around for things to do with my time and thought, 'I know, I'll knit a sweater.' I used to knit as a child, my elder sister taught me, but I hadn't knitted for years and years. I went to the shops to look for a knitting pattern but I couldn't find anything I liked at all. Then one day we were having a quick meal in front of the TV and there was a bottle of HP sauce on the table and I thought — '*That's* what I'd like on my sweater!' (I was rather keen on pop art at the time.) I worked out the design on graph paper — I suppose my maths helped me with that, it's all to do with counting really, and a logical way of thinking — and I worked out a pattern and knitted it up for myself, and wore it. The knitting was *terrible,* and the making-up and everything, but the design was fun. That was my first attempt and I followed it up with a Baked Beans design, then a Coca Cola one, and then I made a Lowry cardigan. All funny little figures and lamp-posts, you know, like the Lowry paintings. I was wearing my Lowry one day when I was shopping in Waitrose, and a lady came up and asked me where I'd found it. When I told her I'd made it she asked me if I'd show it, and any others I had, in an arts and crafts exhibition she was putting on the following Saturday. It was just a little affair really and my husband took me and my sweaters along on the back of his motor-bike, but then the Mayor turned up, and a photographer, and I felt embarrassed, my things were so badly made, so I just put up a little display of them and went home. On the Monday the photographer rang up and said he was from the local paper. The fashion editor had seen his pictures of my sweaters and she wanted to do a little write-up about me, and would that be all right. Well, I agreed, and she came and interviewed me and said she'd put in a small piece, but when I bought the paper I discovered they'd given me the whole of the two centre pages, a huge double spread all to myself. And that was it. That was me launched as a knitwear designer. Off I went to see my bank manager armed with the newspaper, and my sweaters in a garbage bag, and I tipped them out on to his desk and said, 'Now I want you to lend me £300 so that I can buy myself a knitting-machine and do it properly,' He seemed rather amused. He asked me a few questions about 'collateral' I think it was, but I got my loan.

I spent it on a Knitmaster machine which is very good because it has a gadget with which you can punch out your own designs. I spent six weeks teaching myself how to use it and then I decided I'd gone as far as I could go on my own so I got professional tuition from the Knitmaster demonstrator — two hours' tuition and lots of helpful hints. That was marvellous.

KNIT-IN
DOROTHY GREENWOOD
22 Station Road
Berkhamsted
Herts.
Tel 73875

I felt ready to make things professionally then, so I produced a range of children's sweaters. I'd noticed a girl selling children's clothes on a stall in the market — lovely things made from Liberty prints and other beautiful fabrics — and I asked her if she would sell my sweaters too, on a sale-or-return basis, with some commission for herself. She did that and sold them very well. By this time I was getting braver by the minute, so off I went to Naturally British, the shop in Covent Garden, and asked the man there if he'd like to sell my things. He was very interested, but rather than push him into making a quick decision I just told him what sort of price I would want for them, explained that I was going away for a month, and said I'd go to see him again when I got back. Well, I was given a very warm reception on my next visit. He'd sold everything, and one of the sweaters had been selected to go on display in the Design Centre. So he gave me a big order, and also said he'd sell my stuff in his American

branch, in Boston. That sort of thing is very good for you — it really boosts your confidence. I went on from strength to strength. I thought — go for the top. So I took some sweaters to Harrods and got an order, and the buyer at Browns introduced me to an export agent who sold my things to America. Then I went to Paris on a selling trip. I had friends there and they kept saying, 'You must bring your knitwear here and see if you can manage to sell it to the French' — and I did. It was taken on by a firm called Gudule, and Jean Richter asked me to do designs for them, as well.

At that stage it was all going very well, so I got some outworkers, all with their own knitting-machines, and was really busy. Then somehow, last year, the market got more difficult. The competition became intense. Even big stores like Harrods wanted you to provide goods at cheaper and cheaper prices, and started buying in knitwear from Taiwan. And I had a disaster with one firm which took a lot of my things and then went bankrupt, so I didn't get paid. It was then that I decided to get into Knitting Packs — kits including instructions, yarn, charts, buttons and designer's label — and to deal directly with the public, through mail order, as often as I could. I wanted to try my hand at hand-knitting design as opposed to machine-knitting. Again, the maths helped. I actually wrote a computer program for a knitwear design before I'd even *seen* a program. Now I've bought myself a computer and am teaching myself how to use it. When you're working with six different sizes for one design it's amazing how much time it saves, and how accurate it is.

When I decided to move into the knitting-pack business I chose my best-selling design, Canal Scene, which is the view from my window, and turned it into a hand-knitting pattern. A friend drew a picture, a line drawing, of the design, and my 'Knit-In' logo of knitting needles knitting up the name, and I had photocopies made of her graphics. Then I wrote a letter about myself and my kits, saying what I'd done, and where I'd sold, and explaining that there weren't many children's knitting packs on the market and I was hoping to fill the gap with my mail order business. Next I made a list of all the magazines and newspapers I thought might be interested, the

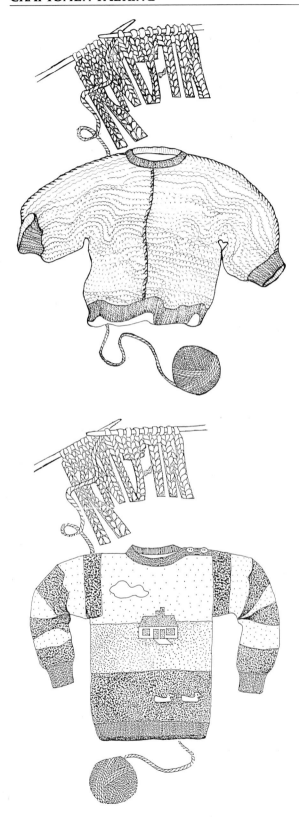

sort that have 'What's New?' type columns, along with the names of their fashion editors. Then I sent the letter and the design to all these people, and sat back and waited to see what would happen. The *Guardian* was the first to give me some coverage, and from their little paragraph on the women's page I got 200 orders in two weeks. Then in every one of the following eleven months I was featured in some magazine — *Mother, Woman's Realm, Parents, Mother and Baby, Pins and Needles,* and lots more.

The piece in *Mother* got me 130 orders *and* they asked me to do patterns for the magazine too, a children's sweater for the April issue, and a baby's outfit for June. There are unexpected spin-offs from publicity, you see. Liberty's saw the piece about me in *Pins and Needles* and as a result of that I'm working with them on the project of providing knitting packs for children's wear in their beautiful new yarn department.

Editorial coverage is *so* much more useful than advertising. I put a little ad in the *Observer* and I'm getting six requests for *leaflets* each day, but from the write-ups I get hundreds of firm *orders*. Besides, editorial mention is free but advertisements are very expensive. The *Observer* cost me £100 for an advertisement every Sunday for a month. But I think you just get featured if you're new, if you're producing something a bit different, and if the editor likes your design. The other thing I've learned is that if you show just one design it seems to attract more of a response than several. My first press release was just one design — Canal Scene. My new leaflet illustrates six — two ladies' packs, Mohair Magic and Comfy, and four for children, Cat, Train, A Day By The Sea and In The Country. The editors don't seem to be showing as much interest in the latter, but it may be because it's my second time round and they're more interested in new people.

Two magazines have asked me if I'd like to do a special offer through them. The way it works is that you pay for the photograph they use, and then they take a percentage of the money you earn. But I'm not sure about that — it doesn't seem very satisfactory to me. You do have to be careful not to make expensive mistakes. I saw an advertisement in the *Observer* Business Section by a firm which sold you mailing lists. I asked if they had one which covered private addresses, families with children, and I was told I could buy 2,500 suitable names. I could only afford to pay for 1,000, at a cost of £48. I sent off a cheque and had hundreds of leaflets and patterns printed and got myself involved in a lot of expense — and then the advertiser vanished without trace. It seemed a reputable firm, being in the Business Section of a paper like the *Observer* for four weeks running. It never even occurred to me that it wasn't genuine, but that was money wasted.

It's a good idea to make contact with the commercial spinners. They are now being influenced by the good work being done by designers and their own patterns are getting better and better. I did a deal with Wendy Wools which I use a lot. I

suggested that I should put an advertisement in the *Sunday Times* promoting my designs and their yarn, and they agreed to pay half the cost of that. Now I'm toying with the idea of trying to sell my patterns to the spinners, to find out whether that is a worthwhile exercise.

I know it sounds as if I'm doing quite well, despite the mistakes, but I'm still not making much money out of my business. Perhaps I'm not as efficient as I should be. I may not be doing my marketing properly. There's so much to learn. Really you just have to work very hard and hope it's going to pay off in the end. I'm always looking for new ideas. My latest is to write a book about designing knitwear for children. There are lots of books about adult knitwear design, but not so many about children's. I really think there's room for that — I'd like to have a go.

PAT JOHNSTON
Fashion Designer
'Handmade'

I trained originally as a window-dresser in Edinburgh and Glasgow. But then I came to live in Caithness — my home was in Kirkwall in the Orkneys, when I was growing up — and of course there is no call for proper window-dressing in a country area like this, so I started working as a craftsman, making blouses, skirts and scarves, all sorts of things, in Harris tweed, wools, cottons and silks. I need to produce a variety of things, not just concentrate on one or two items, because I sell mainly through a retail outlet and you have to give the customers as much to choose from as possible. If I sold mainly through mail order it would be different — then I might make just a few specialised items. As it is, I make clothes, I hand-paint things I've made, and I also paint tee-shirts and sweat shirts that I've bought in.

I work from my home in Gillock. I have a workshop there, and I used to sell from home and through craft fairs and exhibitions. I belong to two crafts organisations, the Caithness Crafts Association and the Caithness Guild of Artist-Craftsmen.

I got to know some of the other crafts people who went to the fairs quite well, and a few of us decided we needed a bigger and more central outlet — the fairs and our workshops weren't really enough. One day I was talking about this problem to a lady I met and she said she had premises next to her house that were standing empty, so five of us took the plunge and rented them for a trial period, just for two months, November and December. That gave us the experience of running a shop, and we enjoyed it and it was a success, so once Christmas was over we started looking for somewhere permanent. We eventually found a nice little place in Princes Street in the centre of Thurso, and three of the original group of five took it over. One of us is a potter, one specialises in knitwear, and I do the fashions.

We called the shop HANDMADE, because everything in it *is*. It's not really a co-operative — it's really four separate businesses, with four separate business accounts and sets of books, all operating under one roof. Each of us has our own individual business, and the shop itself is a business and buys and sells crafts from other craftspeople working all over the country. In this way we can sell lovely silver and wooden items, and jewellery, to add to our own range. But we only stock those things we all consider to be of good quality and craftsmanship, and which will complement our own products.

Although we are not a co-operative we do have to co-operate a great deal, though funnily enough we hardly ever see each other. We leave long notes — we're all great note-writers — and we telephone each other quite a lot. We organise it so that the shop is manned on a rota system. Each one of us does Monday, Tuesday or Wednesday, we close on Thursday, and then we share out the Fridays and Saturdays in turn. We take turns doing the cleaning and dressing the window too. And if anyone is ill or away on holiday, the other two organise it between themselves to cover for her. It ticks over quite neatly. We all get together for a meeting once a month, and that is when we make decisions, work out what we're going to buy, and thrash out all our problems. It's useful that there are three of us because that means there can always be a majority decision. On the other hand, if one person feels very strongly about something, if she really doesn't want to buy a certain item because she doesn't think it's right for HANDMADE, then the other two accept that and don't force the issue.

We get on very well together. We're not always socialising together, but that's quite deliberate, I think. It's easier to be objective and business-like if you're professional partners rather than emotionally involved. We do have arguments, but not rows. We all make a real effort to be sensible and understanding. The thing is, we all have something to gain. We all want the shop to keep going, and we want to be in it. We don't want to be forced to leave through ill-feeling or unpleasantness so there's no point in being awkward or unreasonable. There's too much at stake for squabbles, too much to lose.

Financially, we go thirds on the rent and rates, and the shop pays for the electricity. But if we have a good week we might give ourselves a little treat and let the shop pay the rent. We've never needed to get a loan from the bank, not even an overdraft, but I'm sure we could get one if we needed it, now that we've proved ourselves.

When I started my business I got a small grant from the Highlands and Islands Development Board — not a lot, just enough to buy the equipment I needed. I have an industrial sewing-machine and an overlocker, and I use a fusing press for bonding the interfacings and doing permanent pleating. That also sets dyes more easily and quickly, so it's very useful. All the things I make are made on industrial machines, otherwise they would take so long that it would be impossible to charge a realistic price for them. I have one worker, not an *out*worker. She comes to my house one day a week because that's where the machines are. She's not a home dressmaker, she's an industrial machinist. My work is quite different from home dressmaking, you see. There's no pinning or tacking — it's a totally different technique.

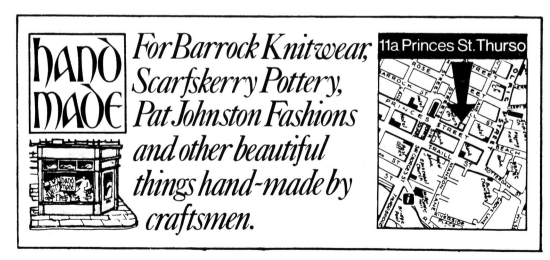

HANDMADE has been going for eighteen months now and at present it's doing well. We have a five-year lease, with a rent review after the first three years. We had a solicitor to help us sort all that out. I don't know what we'll do when the five years are up. We may renew the lease, or we may decide to give it up. Who knows what the future holds? We've got enough to think about just going on from month to month.

I have two children to cope with. At present, the boy is 10 and the girl, 13. They're both very artistic, and my daughter is particularly interested in the business. She would like to come into it herself when she's old enough, and that might be a possibility. They're old enough to look after themselves pretty well now and they don't make many demands on my time, but all the same, I do find that I have to work in the evenings to get everything done.

I still do a few craft fairs at Christmas time, mainly as a form of advertising for the shop. It's not what you sell at the fairs that is important so much as the amount of interest it creates. We all have little advertising leaflets about ourselves, and the Guild of Artist-Craftsmen has a pamphlet about us too. The Guild is quite new. It was formed in 1979 by the craftsmen themselves, to promote the members' work, and it includes weavers, potters, puppet-makers, a jeweller, glass-engraver, and landscape artist. I suppose there are quite a lot of craftspeople up here considering the size of the population. This promotional material that is printed gets distributed all over the place. We have it in the shop, take it to fairs and exhibitions, put it in pubs and all round about. In the tourist places too. But the nice thing is that though you might think it's the holiday-makers who keep us going we really do very well locally. The people who live here are very supportive, so we *don't* have to rely on a seasonal tourist trade. We have no completely slack times. October might be quite quiet, and February isn't very special, but we get through January well because our potter has a sale and the knitwear and clothes go well with people spending their Christmas present money or wanting something warm to see them through the rest of the winter. Basically, there's always money coming in. It's very reassuring.

At the moment I'm quite happy just chugging along. With my family and my husband to look after my hands are tied. There's no point in getting carried away and going all out, because I *want* to spent time with them. Perhaps later, when the children leave home . . . well then, we'll see.

BRIDGET LAPSLEY
Smock-maker
'Flocks & Smocks'

I call my business 'Flocks and Smocks' because it's everything to do with *sheep*. Sheep are the theme, and I use a sheep as my logo on my advertising material.

I sell specialist wools and yarns, hand-knitted sweaters, and particularly the traditional English smocks which are my special thing, and which I produce in four or five designs for both adults and children, hand-made or machine-made, in various weights of calico.

It's quite interesting, the way I began my fascination for smocks. I was working in the wardrobe department for the film of *Far From The Madding Crowd*, on location in Dorset. That's where I saw my first smocks. The real thing. Quite beautiful. It broke my heart the way we had to treat them. They had to be artificially 'broken down', you know, made to look real, and used, and worn, before the actors put them on.

The world Thomas Hardy paints, that particular historical period, is one I feel very much in sympathy with. I find a rural way of life very attractive, and to me that film portrayed a super way of living, so I suppose Thomas Hardy was responsible for the fact that I am now deeply immersed in sheep-things! His books tell us a great deal about smocks. In both *Far From The Madding Crowd* and *Under The Greenwood Tree* he describes in detail the patterns and the different types of fabric that are used, the

Flocks and Smocks

HANDSPINNING AND WEAVING
SPECIALIST YARNS FOR HANDKNITTING
HAND-MADE SMOCKS

*50 High Street
Holt
Norfolk*

Workshop telephone:
ATTLEBOROUGH 850629

**OPEN
TUES FRI SAT 10·30 am - 4·30 pm
CHRISTMAS TO EASTER SAT ONLY
OUTSIDE SHOP HOURS PLEASE TEL.
ATTLEBOROUGH 850 629**

working smocks and the dress smocks. It's fascinating.

That was my first job, being wardrobe assistant with a film company. Before that I'd done a pre-diploma in art and design at Ipswich and then gone on to Loughborough College of Art, where I trained as a designer. But nothing to do with needlecrafts; my diploma was in '3 Dimensional Design', furniture and wood and things, and I'm also a registered silversmith. I've always made my own clothes, though. My mother was very good at sewing and she taught me.

After my stint as wardrobe assistant I did all sorts of other things. I began to teach and was a lecturer at Lincoln College of Art, in charge of the ceramics department. Then I had a spell as a freelance potter but I was not particularly successful. I went into it in the wrong frame of mind. One needs a tremendous amount of encouragement to get going. After that I married and moved to Newark and again I taught ceramics at the local art college. And then . . . well, it was having children. I took eight years off to be a housewife and travelled overseas with my RAF husband. I had four super years in the Mediterranean and sewed a lot, nothing commercial, just for family and friends, but there were superb markets out there selling slight seconds, off-cuts and discontinued lines from Heals and Liberty's, and they were too good to miss out on, so I kept my hand in.

We came back to the UK at the end of '78 and knew we were going to be spending a few years in Norfolk, so we decided to put down semi-permanent roots in the feudal village of Hardingham. I also wanted to buy some property on the north Norfolk coast to let to summer visitors. Before I was married I had bought a cottage in Yorkshire — two up, two down, for which I paid £1,700 — so I sold that and found something in the little town of Holt, tucked away right at the end of the main street. It had been a shop downstairs with living accommodation above, so I decided to keep it like that. I know it sounds the wrong way round. I suppose most people decide they want to open a shop and then begin to look for premises, but I found the premises and then decided I'd like to run a shop. So now I let the upstairs to holiday-makers, and run my business from downstairs. We've been going for two years, opening three days a week, Tuesday, Friday and Saturday, from 10.30 am till 4.30 pm. Last year I opened on Saturday only between Christmas and Easter, but this year I'm going to keep open for the three days and see how I get on. My mother has always helped me in the shop but she wants to be less tied now so she's gradually beginning to take a back seat.

We started off, basically, with hand-spun, hand-knitted items that my mother and I made, and also specialist yarn for hand-knitters. As I say, the theme of the shop is sheep — though the occasional goat creeps in with mohair and alpaca — so the local blacksmith makes us shepherds' crooks to which I attach the wooden shafts. And then we started with fleeces and spinning wheels. The smocks just *happened*. I'd always wanted to make them, so I did one by hand, as a sampler. It was a ludicrously expensive exercise because I could only make one in a week. It took me 40 to 50 hours and I reckoned I could sell it plain-coloured for £85 or hand-dyed for £95 so it just wasn't economic. You see, in the old days a craftsmen *could* earn a living by practising his skill and selling what he made, but now it's a struggle. You have to work out different ways of doing things, cutting your labour costs, using machines, learning how to diversify. To survive I have to keep my shop open, sell my own work and other goods, such as yarn, and find other marketing outlets too.

Now I use four knitting outworkers and four smocking outworkers to boost my productivity. I always go *to* them. I've trained them myself in special afternoon classes, and prepared samples for them. Visiting them, and getting back and forth to the shop takes up a lot of my time because I live 30 miles away from Holt.

I do my own knitwear designs but in our part of the country there is also a demand for traditional knitwear, Arans and Icelandics, and one of my outworkers does superb Sheringham and Cromer jerseys, which are very special and part of our *local* tradition, so there's a large range of sweaters for customers to choose from.

I have just put my finger into the pie of sheepskin products which are a nice extra, but my shop is tiny so I have space problems and can't diversify too much.

I didn't have any special help — grants, advice, bank loans or anything like that — when I started off, though I'm sure there is help available if you know how to get it. I just began with £300 fiddled from the housekeeping and I've deliberately kept the whole thing small-scale. I know I'd have a bigger turnover if I had a shop in Norwich, but this way I can keep firm control of the whole business and it doesn't get out of hand. I do the book work myself, and my husband is the accountant. We've had to teach ourselves everything and it's made enormous demands on us.

The bank manager eventually let me have an overdraft but I had to work hard to get it. He made me prove my viability. I traded for nearly a year without any help at all and even now all the money that comes in goes straight back into buying stock and paying my workers. All I get is my expenses. Still, Flocks and Smocks is very *young*. The business is only two years old. You shouldn't expect to make money at first — it all has to be ploughed back if it's going to grow properly.

As well as the shop I sell through craft fairs and shows sometimes, but I try to be very selective and go only to those I know will work and be worth while. You have to put an enormous amount of organisation into fairs if they are going to be cost effective. I'm just about to spend a week in the Castle Museum at Norwich, in their Best of British Crafts exhibition, and I'm looking forward to that, but up till now the Royal Norfolk Show has been by far my best form of advertisement. It can generate almost enough work to keep my outworkers busy all through the winter. They're very good though. They never complain if we run into a slack period and there's nothing for them to do. I've heard that some outworkers won't work for you unless you can guarantee them an almost constant flow of work, but mine aren't like that.

I've just sent samples of my traditional English smocks to New York to see how they go down there. The interesting thing about smocks is that they used to be worn as working clothes for poor men but now they are considered fashion garments for affluent women. It will be quite exciting to see how America reacts to them. I could cope with extra orders because my outworkers are so good and reliable, but I don't want the business to escalate too much. As it is, it's small and in control and we can have a proper family life and each do our own thing. The business works round the family — it's not separate, it's part of us. And it's very precious and satisfying. My only ambition is to make it work, and to make it work really well.

ANN WRIGHT
Hairdressing and beauty salon wear
'Gasper'

I married into the hairdressing business — before that I was involved in secretarial work and advertising. My husband and I ran a very good salon in an affluent area with an up-market clientele, and we took great pains to make sure that everything about the salon was in very good taste. Carefully chosen decor, lovely colour schemes, beautiful towels and the nicest possible design of equipment. But we found that the choice of client cover gowns and staff wear was dreadful — nasty nylon that felt awful, and boring colours, not at all the sort of thing that we wanted. I was able to sew myself, I've always made my own clothes and things for other people too, and friends used to say I should make our salon wear myself and that way I would get the sort of quality I was looking for.

After a while my husband had to sell the salon because of severe health problems, but we stayed in touch with the wholesalers we'd worked with, and one of them suggested that I should take the idea of producing and marketing salon wear really seriously. It was obvious that I'd have to take over the responsibility of being chief bread-winner for a while, until my husband was better, so I took up his idea. I started in a very small way because I had a small child and couldn't get totally immersed in business. There is an exhibition at Earls Court every year called Salon International and I plucked up my courage and took space in the bazaar section, showing what I could do. Everything took off from there. I started selling all over the country, and then internationally, and I've gone on expanding ever since.

I couldn't have done it without professional help and advice because despite my secretarial experience I really knew hardly anything about business, so I did a six-month government-sponsored course with LENTA, the London Enterprise Agency. It was marvellous. I can't recommend it too highly. I paid about £200 for the course but that was peanuts compared with the real value which must have been nearer £1,000. I was taught *everything* to do with business practice. I knew nothing at all about manufacturing or costing or things like that and it was all a bit daunting, but they gave me a lot of encouragement. At the end students were introduced to a bank, and were able to put their programme forward and get any facilities they needed. I found it all very interesting. Now I am invited back as one of their success stories, and join a panel to speak to new people going through the training. I enjoyed all that enormously. I did it just after my second child was born and it brought me out of myself. You know how you lose confidence when you've spent a lot of time being involved with young babies — well, they really gave it back to me.

When I began I started with my own money, about £500, and got a bank overdraft for the first year, but now I no longer need it. I've got to the stage where I can even buy my own computer, and that's going to happen very soon. I run the business entirely from home. We have a town house and downstairs there is a double integral garage which we have turned into a workshop, and all the machinery is in there. I have two industrial sewing-machines, a button-holer, a button-sewer, cutting equipment, and racks. Next to the garage is a study which we have turned into the office — that's where we do the paper work and display our range of garments. I choose to work from home rather than from business premises at present because of the children. One is 7 now, the other is 3½. Since I'm here most of the time, and my husband too, the fact that I'm working doesn't disrupt their lives too much. We're here to look after them and it all blends in together. I do try to make sure that I'm a full-time mum as well as a business woman and make the two halves of my life fit in with each other. For instance, I have seven outworkers but I made sure that I got people who lived near my

sons' school so that I can combine taking and collecting the children with taking and collecting work.

I won't pretend it's easy. There are always problems, and it's an uphill struggle. I try to do a lot of work in the morning while the boys are out and that helps, but the telephone never stops ringing at any time and if they're playing up and making a noise while I'm trying to talk business it can be very difficult. Sometimes I feel a slave to the house, living in it *and* working in it. It's a relief to be able to hand over to someone else, my husband, or one of my workers, and have even just a few moments to myself.

I worry about the neighbours too — upsetting them with the noise of delivery vans coming and going. I've got round that one by arranging to have some of my deliveries dropped off to the butcher at the end of the road so that saves them some of the nuisance. Fortunately the machines themselves are very quiet.

My product falls into two areas — client cover gowns and staff wear. For staff I make a simple dress in polyester cotton for easy care, in eight basic colours, red, blue, pink, grey, and so on. For clients I make gowns in eighteen to twenty fabrics, in a whole range of mix-and-match combinations to go with salon colour schemes — sorting out all the possible variations is one of the jobs my computer will be able to help me with.

I have quite a few people working for me now. As well as the seven outworkers I have a girl out on the road selling, and a part-timer who comes in to mark up the garments. And my husband helps with the cutting and the office work as well as sharing with the care of the children.

The main problem is . . . just getting things done. We have frantically busy periods. There are two big hairdressers' exhibitions — the one I mentioned in Earls Court which is held in October, and another in Blackpool in March. After each one there is a great flood of orders. We've become one of the big names in salon wear, and at the last exhibition mine was by far the busiest stand because what I have to offer is the most fashionable and best-designed. Something special. But that success means that we all have to work doubly hard once the exhibition is

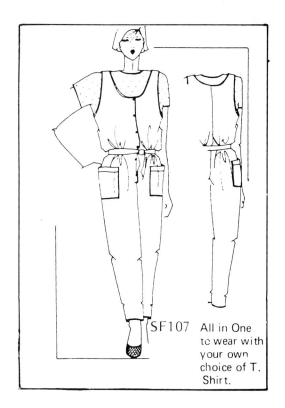

SF107 All in One to wear with your own choice of T. Shirt.

over. I don't take on extra workers because I know the ones I have so well and they're into the swing of things. We just get our heads down and get on with it. But I get totally exhausted. Sometimes I just collapse into bed after supper to get my strength up to face the next day.

You get special problems too. For instance, I'm now making staff dresses for John Lewis in pure white — and that's tricky, making sure they remain pure white while they're being made and transported about the place in my little Renault! And it was difficult to start with finding fabric and threads. At first I was at my wits' end. The people who advertise in the *Yellow Pages* just don't want to know about small businesses, they're only interested in big orders. So I had to start going to the FABREX exhibitions at Olympia and find my own contacts. They're held in March and October, just at the same time as the hairdressers' exhibitions, so you can imagine what it's like trying to find the time to fit them in! At first I was honest and told people I was just a beginner and the wholesalers would look down their noses at me as if I were wasting their time.

Now it's easier because I have built up a name and a reputation, but at the beginning it takes a lot of time and persistence to find the right suppliers, and there's no easy way round it.

Despite all this we've managed to get by. If money was no object I'd probably have bigger premises and employ more people, but I'm not ready for further expansion just yet. Later on perhaps. If all I'm going to do is live just to work there doesn't seem to be any point in it — you have to have a decent *life*. Five years ago I got pushed into having to earn a livelihood because of our family difficulties, and once I started there was no turning back, but I've never wanted it to get out of hand. I want to spend time with my children — I always wanted to have children and be with them, be a proper mother. They'll be grown up soon enough. I'm not ambitious. I feel satisfied with what I've done. The key was to find a hole in the market, and then fill it, and I've done that. It's nice to make progress, but not at the cost of being parted from my children. I could have been bigger by now — but then, I could have made more expensive mistakes. As it is, I make to order, and I get the money with the order, so I don't sit on a lot of stock and I'm pretty safe. I *haven't* needed a huge injection of capital, I *have* created a viable business, and I feel it's mine, my own work. It pays for everything — the house, our food and clothes, the car and school fees. It would be nice to have a little extra for holidays, but one of the things I've learnt is that you can't have everything. I'm very thankful really. It's all been so *interesting!*

KATIA CADMAN
Designer
'Up-front Design'

It's difficult to explain exactly what I do to people who aren't in the entertainment business, but to put it at its simplest, I make drapes for the stage. In one sentence — imagine a stage: everything in fabric on a stage, I can do it.

Take a venue like Wembley Arena. When there's no show on it's like a huge warehouse. Not like a theatre at all. You have to build the stage completely. My job is to create the *walls* of the stage from drapes. And when I do rock and roll concerts I have to make drapes to hide the equipment too. In some venues the sound reflects from the wall, and there is a need for drapes to act as sound baffles. Some groups want a visual theme when they go on tour — they want decorative front curtains, painted gauzes, special effects, so you make appliqués, paint on the drapes, that sort of thing.

The biggest drapes I do are 24 feet wide with a 40 foot drop. I refuse to make them bigger than that because they'd be too heavy, and the riggers have to be able to handle them easily and quickly. If a longer drop is needed I usually put a strip of Velcro along the hems so that two curtains can be fastened together to give the necessary length.

I need to work in a very big room so I can do the cutting on the floor — it's more accurate on the floor when you're working with large quantities of material. Recently when I was painting drapes I had to hire a room with a 30 foot high ceiling, then climb up a rigging tower to reach them once they'd been hung up.

I like to take pains to get the drapes just right. The pinning has to be done just so, and I am very particular that all the side hems are the same size and there's a good deep hem at the bottom.

I also make the bags to put the drapes in for transport and storage. I designed those with the

riggers, and made them so that they could lift out the drapes by the ties on the top and they would unfold themselves. When the show is over and the set is being dismantled the stage crew can simply place the bags underneath the drapes then drop them down so that they fall inside. That way everybody is saved a lot of time and the fabric is kept clean.

You can't train to do this job. There's no training course. You have to learn from someone else. A few years ago I worked for someone who knew the trade and she taught me what it was about. From then on I've been teaching myself, and still am.

I am French, and when I came to England six years ago I was a journalist, writing for French music magazines. Then I married an Englishman and the two situations clashed, marriage and my work. I didn't think I could live in England and write for the French papers, and of course it was not easy, being French, to write for the English papers. I had to make a choice. So, I gave up journalism, did some teaching, made some translations into French, worked for a photographic studio. And then I got involved in stage drapes.

I had always been able to sew. I was educated in a very good French school where sewing was considered a basic skill that every girl should have. Also my grandmother, who is now 97, was a fashion designer. She was very firm that I should do my sewing. She forbade me to have a book until I had done my work. After I had done my sewing, *then* I could read.

One day a friend told me that a lady needed help with making stage drapes and asked me if I'd be interested. I went along, and stayed with her, and learnt the basics — mostly making the 'blacks', simple shapes in black fabric. The cutting is tedious because they *must* hang properly — that is very important. And they are huge areas of fabric to work with. There's nothing artistic about that side of it, it's really hard. But I learnt all about blacks, the names of all the different drapes, and where they go on the stage . . . the basic information. And then . . . well, you buy books, and you learn. Sometimes you get orders and you have to do new things. Gradually you become more specialised. Clients come to you and want something, and it's like being a cook — you try, little by little, and invent things. The show must go on and you must make a look, an effect.

Eight months ago I went into business in partnership with John and Roger, who run 'Up-Front Production'. Their line is building and rigging stages. They need drapes so that they can put the whole thing together, so a drapes concern is complementary to their company. They are well known in the business as riggers, so the idea that a drape maker was joining up with them went down well with the people who organise concerts — they could get the whole package in one go. I moved in with Up-Front Production in their warehouse premises on Wapping Wharf, in a huge attic room at the top of the building, overlooking the Thames. I love the area. It has been run down but now it is being redeveloped and coming to life again. These old wharfside buildings have been renovated and separated into units let out to lots of small companies, and the place is throbbing with activity.

Since I didn't have to find premises for myself, and a lot of the business organisation was provided for me, I didn't apply for grants when I started, but I did have to find some money myself to pay for my sewing-machine — it's a very good one, a Brother industrial model — and for my first lot of fabric. I needed a lot of stock to start off because I hire out *and* sell, so there have to be enough drapes available for people to get what they need. Also, it all has to be kept in perfect condition, spotlessly clean, especially the blacks. Black wool absorbs light, it should be invisible when the lights are shining on it, so you can't have the slightest speck of fluff on it or it will show up and spoil the illusion. So, when they are first made, or used, all the drapes have to be hoovered. And everything must be flame-proofed to meet the British Safety Standard. Sometimes the GLC turns up and wants a sample of fabric for testing. Usually I can buy flame-proofed material but sometimes, if I can't get what I want, I have to flame-proof it myself.

Now I am trying to build up my stock slowly so that I can hire out more and give my customers the best. I'm still a very small concern. Sometimes I manage with only one friend helping me.

When I am busy more friends come in informally to give me a hand. When I've been going for a bit longer I will take people on to the payroll and teach them everything, but I have been so busy since I started that I have never had the opportunity even to show anyone else how to use the machine. And it's not just the sewing. The cutting is just as important, and everything must be pinned perfectly.

I keep my own books but I have an accountant, of course, who comes regularly and takes them away for VAT and tax and so on. All the time I am learning. At some point you have to face a situation and even if you have no training, you just get on with it. When I don't know something I pick up the phone and ask for advice. You just find out — go to libraries, buy books, ring up people who you think will know more than you do. I don't think this is a cut-throat business. There are so few of us in it that we might as well help each other. Once I was stuck because my drapes were being used for a Bob Dylan concert in Holland and they got held up over there when I needed them here, so I hired from one of my competitors. And sometimes they hire from me.

I've done a lot of big-name shows — Cliff Richard, Gary Glitter, Frank Sinatra, the Thompson Twins. The video for the Eurythmics. And lots more. The very first show I did was at the National Exhibition Centre in Birmingham and the management was so impressed with the drapes that were hired that they bought their own set. Then I did 'The Magic of Vienna' at the Barbican. They wanted a rich Viennese look, and it was a rush job. We couldn't find flame-proof material in just the right shades of red and cream so we went to John Lewis and bought beautiful French velvet and flame-proofed it all ourselves. That was long work, but it looked very good, lovely.

Show business is very stressful. You're always working to deadlines. Everybody is in a hurry, and very emotional. Performers can't work without drapes, but managers and designers never think about them till the last minute so it's always a rush, often working round the clock. Sometimes you only have a week to do a whole set and you're working twenty-four hours flat and you go through panics. It can be agony, just worrying about it. But in the end we deliver on time and everything goes right, and then I apologise to everyone for having been so terrible. Sometimes we've made a mistake — of course we have — but we've always managed to correct it.

It is necessary to say 'no' occasionally. You can't be too involved or your creativity falls apart. It affects your whole life, takes over. I lost a few stone when I started. When you're just beginning you've got to put so much into it.

At present I don't go on the road, I'm here, working. But as we get more established I'll increase my hire stock, get more equipment and machines, and employ some people so that I can get out more. I'd also like to do more work for the theatre, be more creative. It would be interesting to study design for the stage — I have lots of ideas about design.

It's been an incredible eight months. I have no regrets about all the time and energy I've put in since I started, but it is *very* hard work. It takes all of you.

Appendices

BOOKS

Business Organisation and Extra Training
Strongly recommended

Brady, Christine. *Sewing and Knitting from Home* (Pelham Books, 1981)

CoSIRA, *Handbook*

— — *Local Crafts Directories*

Crowe, John (ed). *Setting Up A Workshop* (Crafts Council Publication, 1984)

Golzen, Godfrey. *Working For Yourself* (Kogan Page, 1980)

Gray, Marianne. *Working From Home* (Piatkus, 1982)

Popular Crafts. Guide to Good Craft Suppliers

— — *Guide to Special Interest Holidays* (Argus Books, Wolsey House, Wolsey Road, Hemel Hempstead, Hertfordshire HP2 4SS (both regularly up-dated)

Crafts Ideas and Techniques

Angell, Jack (ed). *Lingerie* (David & Charles, 1981)

Auld, Rhoda L. *Tatting* (David & Charles, 1976)

Bruce, Pauline. *Creative Sewing/Fashion Accessories* (Studio Vista, 1979)

*Brittain, Judy. *Good Housekeeping Step by Step Encyclopædia of Needlecraft* (Ebury Press, 1979)

Cardy, Lynn and Dart, Alan. *Maternity Clothes* (Bell & Hyman, 1982)

Clark, Christine Lewis. *The Make-It-Yourself Shoe Book* (Routledge & Kegan Paul, 1979)

Couldridge, Alan. *The Hat Book* (Batsford, 1980)

Dawson, Pam. *The Craft of Crochet* (Hutchinson, 1979)

Emlyn-Jones, Gwen. *Make Your Own Gloves* (Bell & Sons, 1974)

Heafield, Margaret. *Young Dressmaker* (Batsford, 1984)

Hollingworth, Shelagh. *Knitting and Crochet for the Physically Handicapped and Elderly* (Batsford, 1981)

Kinder, Kathleen. *A Resource Book for Machine Knitters* (The Dalesknit Centre, Kirkgate, Settle, North Yorkshire BD24 9BX)

Lorant, Tessa. *The Batsford Book of Hand and Machine Knitting* (Batsford, 1980)

McCall's *New Book of Needle Crafts* (W. H. Allen, 1983)

McMorris, Penny. *Quilting, An Introduction to American Patchwork Design* (BBC Publications, 1984)

Maidment, Margaret. *A Manual of Hand-made Bobbin Lace Work* (Batsford, 1931, new edition, 1984)

Mason, David. *Which? Way To Make Soft Furnishings* (Consumers' Association and Hodder & Stoughton, 1984)

Menkes, Suzy. *The Knitwear Revolution* (Bell & Hyman, 1983)

Ounsworth, Magda and Hamilton, Ann. *Ribbon Flowermaking* (available in the UK only from Hamilworth Floral Products)

Probert, Christina. *Knitting in Vogue, Patterns from the '30s to the '80s* (David & Charles, 1983)

Redmile, Brenda. *Machine Dressmaking* (Batsford, 1984)

*Richards, Ena (ed). *The Great Book of Handicrafts* (Octopus, 1982)

Roberts, Patricia. *Knitting Book* (W. H. Allen, 1983)

— — *Second Knitting Book* (W. H. Allen, 1983)

Smith, June Johnson. *The Soft Toy Collection* (Model & Allied Publications, 1980, Wolsey House, Wolsey Road, Hemel Hempstead, Hertfordshire HP2 4SS)

Wark, Edna. *The Craft of Patchwork* (Batsford, 1984)

There are also three excellent series of needlecraft books which are too extensive to be listed individually, but are so comprehensive and useful that they should not be missed.

The Art of Sewing series (Time-Life Books). Titles include: *The Classic Techniques, Creative Design, Delicate Wear.*

The Batsford Dressmaking books. Titles include: *Making Your Own Dress Patterns, Drawing and Designing Children's and Teenage Fashions.*

The Creative Sewing series (Studio Vista, in association with Singer). Titles include: *Household Linen, Patchwork, Basic Fashion Wardrobe.*

APPENDIX 2

MAGAZINES

Needlecrafts

Crochet Monthly
Crafts: bi-monthly (Crafts Council)
Drapers Record: weekly
Embroidery: quarterly (The Embroiderers' Guild)
Home & Freezer Digest: monthly
Inter-Link creative textile crafts magazine: quarterly
   (Halbar Press, High Green Studio, Arkengarthdale,
   Richmond, North Yorkshire DL11 6EL)
Knitting Machine Digest: bi-monthly
McCalls *Needlework & Crafts:* bi-monthly
Modern Knitting: bi-monthly
Pins & Needles: monthly
Popular Crafts: monthly
Quilters' Guild Newsletter: quarterly
Simplicity Today: twice a year
Slipknot: quarterly (Knitting and Crochet Guild)
Stitchcraft: bi-monthly
Style: twice a year
Vogue Knitting: twice a year
World of Knitting: monthly

General

Brides: bi-monthly
Family Circle: monthly
Good Housekeeping: monthly
Harpers & Queen: monthly
Homes and Gardens: monthly
House & Gardens: monthly
Ideal Home: monthly
Living: monthly
New Homemaker: monthly
Vogue: monthly
Wedding Day: bi-monthly
Woman's Journal: monthly
Woman's Own: weekly
Woman's Realm: weekly
World of Interiors: monthly

APPENDIX 3

USEFUL SOCIETIES AND ORGANISATIONS

Crafts

Please send stamped addressed envelope if writing for information

British Crafts Centre,
43 Earlham Street, Covent Garden, London WC2H 9LD
British Hand Knitting Association,
PO Box CR4, Leeds LS7 4NA
British Sewing, Knitting and Needlecrafts Council,
The Old Vicarage, All Souls Road, Halifax HX3 6DR
British Toy and Hobby Manufacturers Association Ltd,
80 Camberwell Road, London SE5 0EG
British Toymakers' Guild,
4 Ruvigny Gardens, London SW15 1JR
Crafts Council,
8 Waterloo Place, London SW1 4AT
Creative Needlecraft Association,
Gawthorpe Hall, Padiham, Near Burnley, Lancashire
Embroiderers' Guild,
Apartment 37, Hampton Court Palace, East Molesley,
   Surrey KT8 GAU
International Lace Society,
English Director: Jean Pegg, 90 Kimberley Road,
   Southbourne, Bournemouth, Dorset
Knitting and Crochet Guild
22 All Saints Way, Beachamwell, Swaffham, Norfolk
   PE37 8BU
Lace Guild of England,
contact Jane Playford (see Appendix 6) for details
Quilters' Guild,
Parklands Farm, Lower Green, Galleywood, Chelms-
   ford, Essex CM2 8QS
Regional Arts Associations,
addresses from your local library
Ring of Tatters,
1 Carr Street, Birstall, Batley, West Yorkshire WF17
   9DY
Royal School of Needlework,
25 Princes Gate, London SW7 1ZE

APPENDIX 4

EXTRA TRAINING

Rural Crafts Association,
Heights Cottage, Brook Road, Wormley, Godalming, Surrey
Townswomen's Guild (national headquarters),
Birmingham Chamber of Commerce House, 75 Harborne Road, Edgbaston, Birmingham B15 3DA
Women's Institute (national headquarters),
39 Eccleston Street, London SW1W 9NT
Worldwide Machine Knitters' Club,
Unit 22, Springvale Estate, Cwmbran, Gwent NP4 5YQ

Business Organisation

British Standards Institute,
Head Office, British Standards House, 2 Park Street, London W1A 2BS
Business in the Community,
227a City Road, London EC1V 1JU
Citizens' Advice Bureau,
address in your local telephone directory
Co-operative Development Agency,
20 Albert Embankment, London SE1 7TJ
CoSIRA,
141 Castle Street, Salisbury, Wiltshire
Department of Employment (Wages Inspectorate),
7th Floor, BP House, Hemel Hempstead, Hertfordshire HP1 1DW
Industrial Common Ownership Movement,
7–8 The Corn Exchange, Leeds LS1 7BP
LENTA,
69 Cannon Street, London EC4
Low Pay Unit,
9 Poland Street, London W1V 3DG
Small Firms Service:
Freefone 2444

Department of Employment: TOPS courses
Knitwear Design Courses: Michaelmas Cottage, Twineham, West Sussex RH17 5NN
Lady Lodge Arts Centre: Orton Goldhay, Peterborough PE2 0JQ
Local Authorities: Colleges of Further Education and Adult Studies
Missenden Summer Schools (various courses): Missenden Abbey, Missenden, Buckinghamshire
Nelson & Colne College (Creative Needlecraft Association): Gawthorpe Hall, Padiham, Near Burnley, Lancashire BB12 8UA
Styal Workshop (textile courses): Anne Blackburn, Quarry Bank Mill, Styal, Cheshire SK9 4LA
The Earnley Concourse (various fabric crafts, soft toys, quilting, collages, etc): Earnley, near Chichester, Sussex
The English Lace School (lacemaking): 42 St Peter Street, Tiverton, Devon
Townswomen's Guild
University Extra-Mural Departments
Urchfont Manor (City & Guilds courses, creative studies, textiles) plus Home Study, near Devizes, Wiltshire
West Dean College of Crafts, Arts & Music, near Chichester, West Sussex PO18 0QX
Women's Institute, Denman College (patchwork, lacemaking, collage, machine-knitting, embroidery, crafts-selling): for further details contact your local branch or the head office of the WI Federation

APPENDIX 5

SOURCES OF WORK AND OUTLETS

Craft fairs: as listed in crafts magazines

Ember Knitters (who have included in their team the knitters from the disbanded 'Homebound Craftsmen')

Mrs E Brown, 83 Bradwell Road, Longthorpe, Peterborough PE3 6QL

J & P Coats

155 Vincent Street, Glasgow

Patons & Baldwins

Alloa, Clackmannanshire, Scotland FK10 1EG

Sirdar Ltd

Flanshaw Lane, Alverthorpe, Wakefield, West Yorkshire WF2 9ND

Women's Institute markets

APPENDIX 6

SUPPLIERS

Craft Materials

(Always send a stamped addressed envelope when writing for price lists, details, etc)

Beckfoot Mill (soft toy and macramé specialists),

Howden Road, Silsden, Keighley, West Yorkshire BD20 0HA

Brimlake Ltd (fur fabric and soft-toy accessories),

Unit J5, 38–40 Upper Clapton Road, London E5 8BQ

Crimple Craft (quilting, appliqué and patchwork),

White Lodge, Hookstone Road, Harrogate, HG2 8QQ

Dainty Toys (soft-toy specialists),

Unit 35, Phoenix Road, Crowther Industrial Estate, Washington, Tyne & Wear

The Dalesknit Centre (knitting-machines, coned yarns, books, magazines),

Kirkgate, Settle, North Yorkshire

Dryad (general needlecraft supplies),

PO Box 38, Northgates, Leicester LE1 9BU

Fred Aldous (general needlecraft materials),

Department 684, 37 Lever Street, Manchester M60 1UX

Hamilworth Floral Products Ltd, (ribbons, etc, for flower-making),

581 Anlaby Road, Hull, North Humberside HU3 6SH

Handywoman (knitting yarns),

105 High Road, Chiswick, London W4 2ED

Jane Playford (lacemaking accessories and books),

North Lodge, Church Close, West Runton, Norfolk NR27 9QY

John and Pippa Brooker (lacemaking accessories and hand-decorated beads),

Flint Studio, The Square, East Rudham, King's Lynn, Norfolk PE31 8RB

J. W. Coates Ltd (fabrics),
Croft Mill, Foulridge, Colne, Lancashire BB8 7NG
Knitters & Sewers World (soft-toymaking supplies),
21–2 Park Street, Swansea SA1 3DJ
Mace & Nairn (embroidery supplies),
89 Crane Street, Salisbury, Wiltshire
Magpie Patchworks (patchwork, quilting and embroidery supplies),
621 Wimborne Road, Winton, Bournemouth, Dorset BH9 2AR
Mary Allen (embroidery requirements),
Wirksworth, Derbyshire DE4 4BN
Oakley Fabrics (soft-toy materials),
60 Collingdon Street, Luton LU1 1RX
Patchwork Dog & Calico Cat (sewing supplies and cotton fabric),
21 Chalk Farm Road, London NW1
Penelope Wise (knitting yarns),
607 Old Loom House, Back Church Lane, London E1 1LS
Pick 'n' Choose (toymaking, sewing and craft supplies),
56 Station Road, Northwich, Cheshire CW9 5RB
Pioneer Patches (patchwork and quilting supplies),
Inglewood Lodge, Birkby Road, Huddersfield HD2 2DA
Pongees (silks),
184–6 Old Street, London EC1V 9BP
Rowan Yarns (knitting, weaving and needlework supplies),
Green Lane Mill, Washpit, Holmfirth, West Yorkshire HO7 1RW
Russell & Chappel (canvas),
Monmouth Street, London WC2

Strawberry Fayre Fabrics (cotton fabrics and quilting supplies),
Chagford, Devon TQ13 8EN
The Busy Bees (handicraft specialists),
PO Box 14, Camborne, Cornwall TR4 9XD
Wolfins (calico),
Great Titchfield Street, London W1
Wykraft Products (knitting beads and sequins),
8 Tarrant Way, Moulton, Northamptonshire, NN3 1UF
Yarncraft (weaving, spinning and knitting supplies),
Lodge Enterprises, 112A Westbourne Grove, London W2 5RU
Yeoman Yarns (machine-knitting yarns and fabrics),
89 Leicester Road, Kibworth, Leicester LE8 0NP

Labels and Packaging

Able-Label (stick-on labels),
Steepleprint Ltd, Earls Barton, Northampton NN6 0LS
Diverse Marketing (labels of all types),
Westruther, Gordon, Berwickshire TD3 6NE
Mortimer Box Co Ltd (polythene bags),
132 Great Portland Street, London W1N 6DN
Progressive Supplies (Paper) Ltd (packaging material of all sorts),
18 Crawford Place, London W1H 2AJ
R & H King (fabric labels),
19 Tyler's Acre Avenue, Edinburgh EH12 7JE
Wovina (fabric labels),
Bodmin, Cornwall

Index

Numbers in *italic* refer to illustrations